FRANCIS FRITH'S

TENTERDEN - A HISTORY AND CELEBRATION

THE FRANCIS FRITH COLLECTION

www.francisfrith.com

TENTERDEN

A HISTORY AND CELEBRATION
OF THE TOWN

ALEC LAURENCE

THE FRANCIS FRITH COLLECTION

www.francisfrith.com

First published in the United Kingdom in 2004
by The Francis Frith Collection®

Hardback edition 2004 ISBN 1-90493-848-5
Paperback edition 2012 ISBN 978-1-84589-657-7

British Library Cataloguing in Publication Data

Tenterden - A History and Celebration of the Town
Alec Laurence

The Francis Frith Collection®
Oakley Business Park, Wylye Road,
Dinton, Wiltshire SP3 5EU
Tel: +44 (0) 1722 716 376
Email: info@francisfrith.co.uk
www.francisfrith.com

Printed and bound in Great Britain
Contains material sourced from responsibly managed forests

Front Cover: **TENTERDEN HIGH STREET 1900** 44994t

Additional images supplied by Alan Brand.

Domesday extract used in timeline by kind permission of
Alecto Historical Editions, www.domesdaybook.org
Aerial photographs reproduced under licence from
Simmons Aerofilms Limited.
Historical Ordnance Survey maps reproduced under licence from
Homecheck.co.uk

Every attempt has been made to contact copyright holders of
illustrative material. We will be happy to give full acknowledgement in
future editions for any items not credited. Any information should be
directed to The Francis Frith Collection.

*The colour-tinting in this book is for illustrative purposes only,
and is not intended to be historically accurate*

AS WITH ANY HISTORICAL DATABASE, THE FRANCIS FRITH ARCHIVE IS
CONSTANTLY BEING CORRECTED AND IMPROVED, AND THE PUBLISHERS
WOULD WELCOME INFORMATION ON OMISSIONS OR INACCURACIES

Contents

Historical Timeline for Tenterden

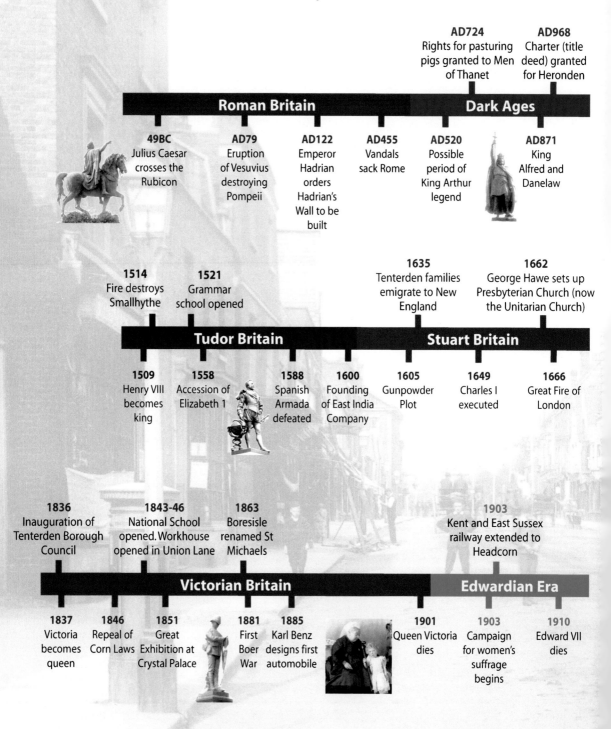

AD724 Rights for pasturing pigs granted to Men of Thanet

AD968 Charter (title deed) granted for Heronden

Roman Britain

Dark Ages

49BC Julius Caesar crosses the Rubicon

AD79 Eruption of Vesuvius destroying Pompeii

AD122 Emperor Hadrian orders Hadrian's Wall to be built

AD455 Vandals sack Rome

AD520 Possible period of King Arthur legend

AD871 King Alfred and Danelaw

1514 Fire destroys Smallhythe

1521 Grammar school opened

1635 Tenterden families emigrate to New England

1662 George Hawe sets up Presbyterian Church (now the Unitarian Church)

Tudor Britain

Stuart Britain

1509 Henry VIII becomes king

1558 Accession of Elizabeth 1

1588 Spanish Armada defeated

1600 Founding of East India Company

1605 Gunpowder Plot

1649 Charles I executed

1666 Great Fire of London

1836 Inauguration of Tenterden Borough Council

1843-46 National School opened. Workhouse opened in Union Lane

1863 Boresisle renamed St Michaels

1903 Kent and East Sussex railway extended to Headcorn

Victorian Britain

Edwardian Era

1837 Victoria becomes queen

1846 Repeal of Corn Laws

1851 Great Exhibition at Crystal Palace

1881 First Boer War

1885 Karl Benz designs first automobile

1901 Queen Victoria dies

1903 Campaign for women's suffrage begins

1910 Edward VII dies

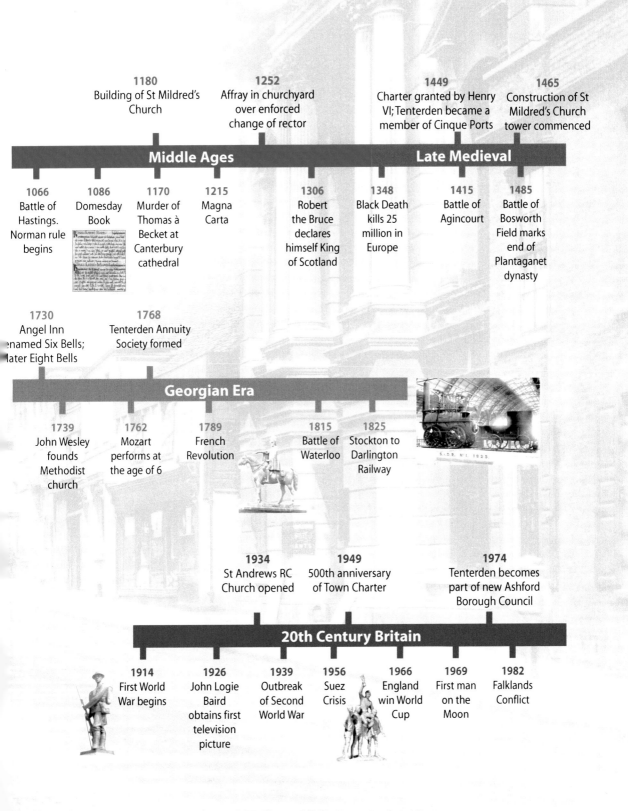

1180
Building of St Mildred's Church

1252
Affray in churchyard over enforced change of rector

1449
Charter granted by Henry VI; Tenterden became a member of Cinque Ports

1465
Construction of St Mildred's Church tower commenced

Middle Ages

Late Medieval

1066
Battle of Hastings. Norman rule begins

1086
Domesday Book

1170
Murder of Thomas à Becket at Canterbury cathedral

1215
Magna Carta

1306
Robert the Bruce declares himself King of Scotland

1348
Black Death kills 25 million in Europe

1415
Battle of Agincourt

1485
Battle of Bosworth Field marks end of Plantaganet dynasty

1730
Angel Inn renamed Six Bells; later Eight Bells

1768
Tenterden Annuity Society formed

Georgian Era

1739
John Wesley founds Methodist church

1762
Mozart performs at the age of 6

1789
French Revolution

1815
Battle of Waterloo

1825
Stockton to Darlington Railway

1934
St Andrews RC Church opened

1949
500th anniversary of Town Charter

1974
Tenterden becomes part of new Ashford Borough Council

20th Century Britain

1914
First World War begins

1926
John Logie Baird obtains first television picture

1939
Outbreak of Second World War

1956
Suez Crisis

1966
England win World Cup

1969
First man on the Moon

1982
Falklands Conflict

CHAPTER ONE

Early History up to 1449

THERE IS little early history of Tenterden recorded, largely because of its geographical position in the vast forest areas between the Thames and the south-east coast of Britain. In this particular area, the forest swept down to the northern edge of a very large sea estuary into which the River Rother flowed. It is contended that in pre-Roman times, the only inhabitants were the itinerant iron workers who moved from site to site along trackways of their own making when the supplies of iron ore became exhausted.

During the later invasion by the Romans, whose base was Rutupiae (Richborough), the main route of the occupying forces was Watling Street, which went along the Thames Estuary to Londinium. However, the Romans did penetrate the forest areas, which they called Anderida, mainly by improving the iron workers' trackways. There is evidence of a Roman road from Benenden to Ashford and thence to Canterbury, which went through the area north of what became Tenterden (see page 10) - sections of this road can still be walked today.

But only a few relics of the Roman occupation have been found in the Tenterden area, mostly near Reading Street, the most notable one being the Mithraic stone in Stone churchyard. One prominent location in this area over the centuries has been Morghew, which some consider to be derived from the Latin word for a burial place. Consider the American slangword for mortuary!

ROMAN TRACKWAYS, THE TENTERDEN TAPESTRY ZZZ00235	THE ORIGINS, THE TENTERDEN TAPESTRY ZZZ00236	ST MILDRED'S TOWER, THE TENTERDEN TAPESTRY ZZZ00239

(Reproduced by kind permission of the Tenterden Museum)

The Ancient Coastline and
the River Rother

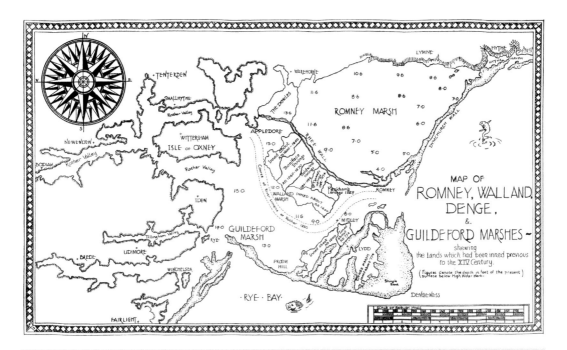

MAP OF ROMNEY, WALLAND, DENGE AND GUILDFORD MARSHES ZZZ00003

(Reproduced by kind permission of the Tenterden Museum)

During the Roman period, the River Limen of those days was flowing south-east to the sea and the settlement of Portus Lemanis, near today's Lympne. After the Romans left, the Limen appears to have silted up or been blocked by longshore drift of shingle, and Romney Marsh began to take shape. Embankments were made to keep out the influx of the sea at high tides, and in the 12th century, grants of land carried provision for tenants to maintain these embankments. The river (now called the Rother) made its way from Appledore to New Romney, and to aid this movement of water, it was converted into a canal. During the 13th century, a series of storms led to a rise in sea level: these storms occurred in 1236, in 1250 (when Old Winchelsea was overwhelmed by the sea) and in 1287, a particularly violent one which altered the coastline. The river from Appledore now turned south, flowing through the inundated lands around Rye and thence out to sea.

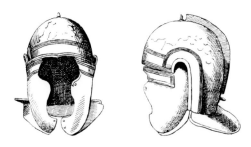

ROMAN HELMET F6014

When the Romans left Britain, the land in part of the south east was settled by the Jutes, whose name for this area was Kant (corner), from which are derived Cantium, Cantiana, and indeed Kent. They called the forest Andredsweald (the name was shortened in later times to Weald), and they used the Roman roads as droveways to clearings in the forest used for the communal pasturing of pigs. These were called 'drofdens', and here the pigs grazed on acorns. The term was shortened to 'dens', hence the predominance

THE ROMAN ROAD FROM BROWNS CORNER 2004 T24701k (Alan Brand)

Did you know?

Roman Roads

Apart from Watling Street from Thanet to London, the most important road was between Rochester and Hastings. At Amber Green near Maidstone a branch route ran to Portus Lemanis (Lympne), a harbour on the south-east coast. Joining these two roads was a minor one from Benenden to a point south of Ashford, which carried on to Canterbury (Durovernum). Part of the latter may be walked today from Millpond Lane to St Michaels, where it bisects the churchyard before carrying on to Woodchurch and Ashford.

wedding night'. After the arrival of Augustine at Canterbury in 597AD, Christianity gradually spread throughout Kent until eventually the church authorities owned a good proportion of the land. Charters (title deeds) were granted for the building of manor houses on such land; those relevant to Tenterden are Ashenden (833), Huson (843) and Heronden (968).

After the Norman Conquest, land tended to be granted to William's closest allies, and afterwards to their descendants. The Domesday Book reflects the church's ownership of the land, as there is no mention therein of Tenterden or of surrounding locations such as Rolvenden. All land within the Canterbury Diocese in church ownership was shown en bloc. Otherwise little recorded history of the Norman period is available; it

ARTIST'S IMPRESSION OF SAXON HOUSES F6015

of Wealden locations ending in this suffix. The Jutish lands were divided into large areas called lathes, and at first only those living in lathes which had forest areas were allowed to graze their pigs. But in a charter of 724, the King gave pasturing to men from other lathes. These included Thanet, from whence men came to the Tenterden area, which in those days was called Brentingsleag. Soon the name was altered to Tenet-wara-den (meaning 'Thanet-men of-pig pasture'), from which, after many decades and some 50 different spellings, is derived today's name for the town.

Some authorities for this period contend that Morghew was derived from the Saxon word 'morgenifu', literally translated as 'the dowry given to a bride the morning after the

is quite a time later, in 1180, that one learns of the building of St Mildred's Church - the first completed sections were the nave and chancel. The south aisle was added in the 13th century and the north aisle in the 14th. The dedication of the church to St Mildred is appropriate in view of the town's existence stemming from the men of Thanet. Mildred

HIGH STREET c1950 T24023

This photograph shows the different widths of the High Street, and illustrates where shops have encroached on the King's Highway (see page 14).

The Heronden Charter of AD986

A translation of this document reads: 'This is the agreement that Aelfwold and Eadwold have agreed, that is that Aethelflaed and Eadwold give to Aelfwold one den in return for the agreed payment which she has received, that is MCCCCL pence. This den is named HYRINGDAENN (the boundaries of the land are stated in detail) to have and to hold happily in his lifetime to be enjoyed in perpetual inheritance and after his day to have power to leave it to whatever heir he shall please, free in every way. If anyone indeed, which we do not desire, or the servant of anyone, instigated by the rashness of the devil, shall arise and shall be tempted to infringe or diminish this my gift and munificence, or to in any way upset what has been agreed by us, let him know himself arraigned before the tribunal of the highest and eternal justice by Almighty God and cut off from the society of all saints, unless before this in this present lifetime he shall be willing to make amends to God and to all men with proper and sufficiently acceptable deeds.' The charter was signed by King Edgar himself, Archbishop Dunstan and other prominent churchmen.

was the daughter of Queen Bertha, the first person to be converted to Christianity by Augustine. Princess Mildred became a nun at Minster Abbey, rising to the rank of Abbess.

The first incumbent at St Mildred's in 1180 was Hugo Norman; he was presented by the Abbot of St Augustine's and endorsed by the Pope, a procedure which largely continued until the Reformation in 1533. Not that this system was infallible: after Peter de Depenham was appointed to St Mildred's in 1250, he was replaced by Henry de Wingham a year later at the behest of Pope Innocent Ill himself. The change of incumbent proved very unpopular with some of the parishioners. The rival parties became involved in a riot in the churchyard, during which Henry of Smallhythe was killed. About the same time an event occurred which quite literally shaped the future of the town. Alexander of Tenwardine (the current spelling at the time!) and two others decided to erect seven shops near St Mildred's Church. To

avoid building them in the churchyard itself, they elected to move the location a few yards to the south. In doing so, they laid themselves open to a charge of 'encroaching on the King's highway'; they were brought up before the Shire Court and found guilty of the charge. However, they were allowed to continue using the shops on condition that an annual fee of twelve horseshoes was paid to the King. This fee (which was later commuted to a money payment of rents) was paid throughout the centuries right up to 1969, when the total payment of 6s 8d was considered too small to be worth collecting. There are now more modern shops along the same stretch of land. These shops are the reason why the present-day High Street is narrower here than the remainder of its length (see T24023). As Tenterden entered the medieval period, it was growing in size and importance, and was being recognised as one of the Seven Hundreds of the Weald. The term 'hundred' dates from Saxon times, and has several definitions. The OCD defines it as an administrative district, but does not qualify this as to size or population. My own preference is to define it as the area of land which could sustain 100 families. Each hundred was controlled by a bailiff appointed by the King, and responsible for collection of taxes and local justice. He was required to hold a court every third week throughout the year, in the open air! Any serious charge such as murder, or cases he could not rule on, were referred to the Shire Court at Penenden Heath near Maidstone. To assist the bailiff in his task, the hundred was divided into 6 'boroughs', each with a reeve who administered justice on minor charges and helped in tax collection. The names of these boroughs, Town, Castweazle, Shrubcote, Dumbourne, Boresisle and Reding, remained in use for centuries – indeed, they appear in the 19th century Census records. Moreover, parts of modern Tenterden still bear the names of most of them (see ZZZ00004).

There are varying opinions as to the reason for Tenterden's location in those earlier days. A H Taylor, the 19th-century antiquarian, took the view that the development of Tenterden from a number of

forest dens into a town was probably due to a great extent to the desire of St Augustine's Abbey, the landlords, to encourage a market at the meeting point of several early highways. The ancient track along the northern edge of Romney Marsh through Woodchurch climbed onto the High Weald up Clay Hill, meeting the road from the river port of Appledore at Golden Square, and thence

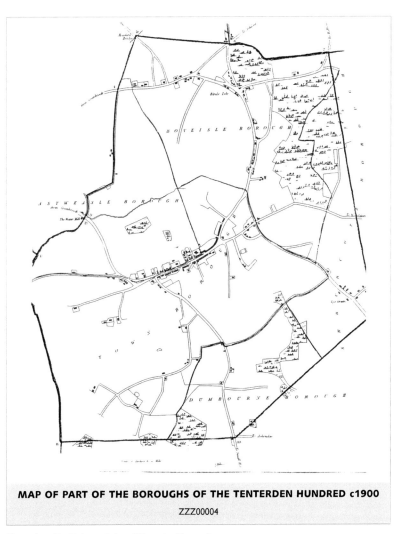

MAP OF PART OF THE BOROUGHS OF THE TENTERDEN HUNDRED c1900

ZZZ00004

(Reproduced by kind permission of Tenterden Museum)

TENTERDEN, FROM THE AIR 1958   AFA71338

stretched along the dry ridge to West Cross. From there, it went either to Cranbrook or down to the bridge over the Ashbourne stream and on to Rolvenden and Newenden, the ancient market town on the River Rother. The ridge between East Cross and West Cross was ideally situated for a town's development, with a plentiful supply of water available from shallow wells on either side. The evidence of existing 15th-century buildings suggests that the early development of the High Street was concentrated near St Mildred's Church, with some dwellings on the southern side of the ridge towards West Cross, and others on the northern side, such as Pittlesden Manor with its farm and orchards.

However, Hasted, the 18th-century historian of Kent, maintained that 'most of the road from the town to Smallhythe, particularly the upper part of it known as Broad Tenterden, is said to have been lined with buildings on each side, and to have been the most populous part of the parish'. Whatever its exact location, Tenterden had its share of medieval hall houses. At that time, housing varied from the wealthy landowners' manor houses to the hovels lived in by the very poor. But the yeomen and wealthier tradesmen were able to reside in the hall houses, which were basically one very large room with a lofty ceiling above. There was a central hearth on the stone floor, and the smoke from its fire rose up and was supposed to leave the room by means of a hole left in the gable end. All through the year, the family, the servants and probably the animals lived together in this type of house, although in later years there was a practice

THE GATEHOUSE OF PITTLESDEN MANOR ZZZ00010

(Reproduced by kind permission of Tenterden Local History Society)

for a bedroom to be constructed on an upper floor for use at night by the husband, his wife and the youngest child. Hall houses date from the 13th century onwards, but by the 16th century there was a tendency for upper floors to be built, together with fireplaces and

chimney stacks. There are several examples of altered buildings in Tenterden, the Tudor Rose (now the Lemon Tree) being the most recognisable one (see 44998, page 20). There are, however, several unaltered ones, which may be seen in the Weald and Downland Museum at Singleton.

By the 14th century, there were signs of increasing differences between the King and the Archbishop over land and monetary matters, including one instance where the Abbot of St Augustine's overruled the nomination of the King's choice for Vicar of Tenterden. There is only a small mention

OLD HOUSE IN HIGH STREET 1900 44998

This house was formerly called The Tudor Rose, and is now The Lemon Tree. It is an example of a hall house altered in the 16th century.

of the Black Death of 1348 in this area and its effect on Tenterden folk; but the poll tax to raise funds for the continuing war against France aroused anger here, and eventually led to the Wat Tyler revolt of 1381. This unpopular poll tax, plus other excessive levies, led to the non-payment of these and the rise in the number of outlaws. But in some cases the outlaws received pardons in return for the payment of fines. The general unrest culminated in the Jack Cade rebellion of 1450.

However, one part of Tenterden was by the 14th century beginning to become prosperous: this was Smallhythe, where shipbuilding was being developed. The River Rother in those days flowed both north and south of the Isle of Oxney, and the northern branch was sufficiently deep for ships to be built and launched at Smallhythe. It was a very industrious place, and apparently rose in importance to become the premier ship-building location in the whole of the country for the next two centuries. This tends to be confirmed by the record of Henry V's visit to supervise the building of his ships which transported his army to France for the campaign which ended in victory at Agincourt. Later, in 1421, it is reported that the King granted a life pension of 4d a

SMALLHYTHE, THE PRIEST HOUSE 1900 45007c

SMALLHYTHE, THE PRIEST HOUSE 1902 49085

day to John Hoggetynes, a master carpenter, 'because in labouring long about them (the ships) he is much shaken and worsten in body'. The necessary timber and iron required for this industry were of course readily available from the Wealden forest. It is hard to imagine when one visits the present day Smallhythe that it was once a thriving area of 200 houses, including the harbour-master's house, now Smallhythe Place, owned by the National Trust. All but two of these houses were destined to be burnt down or severely damaged in a terrible fire in 1514; one of the buildings affected was the chapel, which had only been erected in 1509.

The industry continued to thrive throughout the Tudor period, as is shown by the construction in 1545 of a 'great galleon' of 300 tons to be manned by 250 men, and the rebuilding of the King's ship 'Grand Masters',

Did you know?

Shipbuilding at Smallhythe

In the 1990s, the Channel 4 Time Team party visited the Smallhythe area in an attempt to establish exactly where the shipbuilding took place. It had previously been thought that the likely site was Delph Marsh, a rectangular area; but Time Team's modern technology and basic digging methods resulted in Delph Marsh being discarded in favour of a location near Smallhythe Place, the harbour-master's house in medieval times. The team's finds are exhibited in the Town Museum.

(Reproduced by kind permission of the Tenterden Local History Society)

SMALLHYTHE, ST JOHN'S CHURCH AND THE WAR MEMORIAL ZZZ00006

400 tons with 250 men, which was launched in 1549. The silting-up of the Rother, which was partly due to the unauthorised discharge of ballast from visiting vessels, led to Smallhythe being closed down soon after this, but such was the status of the key workers that they were moved to Woolwich, which gradually assumed the mantle of the premier shipbuilding location. Smallhythe, in addition to Reading Street and Appledore, was also a port used for the export of timber from the Wealden forest.

At about the same period as when Smallhythe's shipbuilding was at its height, a further area of prosperity was being developed in Tenterden itself: the cloth-making industry. Wool from sheep farmed on the nearby Romney Marsh was readily available. It was spun and woven into woollen broadcloth, after which it was washed and processed at the several fulling mills in and around the town. The washed cloth was hung out to dry on plots of land referred to as tenterfields and stretched on tenterhooks. These names have on occasions been erroneously assumed to relate to the name of the town. As early as May 1337, King Edward III had issued an edict to encourage Flemish cloth workers to reside in England. Kent was selected as the seat of the broadcloth manufacture, and the Weald acquired a reputation for making strong durable broadcloth of good mixtures and colours. One other notable location for this industry was Cranbrook. Wealthy clothier families became established in Tenterden and added much to the prosperity of the town. The names of Tilden, Skeets and several others were to be amongst the prominent clothier families in later centuries. The 15th century was probably the most affluent period in the whole of Tenterden's history; it brought about several important events - the main one happened in 1449.

On 1 August 1449, the town and hundred of Tenterden was granted its Charter by King Henry VI. The charter altered the status of the town from being a member of the Seven Hundreds of the Weald to joining the Cinque Ports Confederation, and a translation of an extract from it reads as follows:

'... that from St John the Baptist next the said Town and Hundred of Tenterden be incorporate of a Bailiff and the Commonalty thereof, who shall have a perpetual succession, able to acquire lands and other possessions, having a common seal and capable of pleading and being impleaded in any court, and the inhabitants, tenants and residents on the said feast from year to year shall choose of themselves a Bailiff of good governance of the Town and Hundred who shall hold a court before himself or his deputy within the town a fortnight after St John the Baptist next, and so fortnightly, to hear and determine all pleas of all trespasses, conventions, contracts and other matters, and pleas of withernam and of land and tenures within the Town and Hundred; and they shall have cognizances of the same pleas and the executions thereof, and the fines, amercements and ransoms therefrom ... and the Bailiff and Commonalty shall be quit of all toll and custom whatsoever of shires and hundreds ... that the said Town and Hundred

The Cinque Ports Confederation

BARONS OF THE CINQUE PORTS CARRYING THE CANOPY OVER THE MONARCH ZZZ00005

(Reproduced by kind permission of the Tenterden Museum)

The confederation is thought to date from Saxon times; the original five ports (hence cinque) were Sandwich, Dover, Hythe, Romney and Hastings, which were joined later by two 'Ancient Towns', Rye and Winchelsea. In return for providing ships for the King's service, they were exempt from taxes and tolls, but they also enjoyed other privileges. Boats from these ports could land fishing catches at Yarmouth in Norfolk to sell the produce there, the right of den and strand. After much opposition from the Norfolk men, the King intervened to stop the practice. Another privilege introduced in 1141 allowed the Barons of the Cinque Ports to carry a canopy over the monarch being crowned and to attend the subsequent banquet in the Great Hall, Westminster. This was stopped after the coronation in 1820 when the Barons unfortunately dropped the canopy on George IV, but was reinstated to some degree in 1901 when they were allowed to carry a flag each of an Empire country. Outstanding differences between the members were dealt with at the Court of Shepway, and periodic meetings were arranged at Brodhull (near Dymchurch) for members of head ports, and at Guestling for lesser members. The mayors today carry on this tradition under the title of Brotherhood and Guestling.

TUDOR SHIP F6022

prosperity had considerably declined because that town had 'come to such waste and poverty by the tides and burnings committed by the enemies that neither the town nor the Barons and good men thereof can find their contingent of the (Cinque Ports) fleet'. In return for ship service, Tenterden enjoyed the same privileges as her head port. These included, among others, complete freedom from all taxation, duties and tolls and a person's right of being tried only within the town's own courts. By virtue of an agreement with Rye, Tenterden was required to supply one of the ships demanded of Rye together with its crew of 24 men, and to pay a fixed yearly sum of six marks (£4) to her, as well as to contribute towards the expenses of the courts of Brotherhood and Guestling. Over the years there were many controversies between the two towns regarding Tenterden's financial contribution, which were only resolved with Rye's unsuccessful lawsuit in 1765.

Government was by a Bailiff (who was ex-officio the coroner) and Jurats; the corporate body was known as the Bailiff and Commonalty. Administration was in accordance with a set of bye-laws and decrees known as the Custumal. The Bailiff was elected by the freemen (all males over the age of 12 years) at the common assembly held in the churchyard on 29 August each year. If a duly elected Bailiff refused to accept office, he was fined £10; if he was unable to pay the fine, then the freemen could proceed

shall be incorporated in the Town of Rye and separate from the County of Kent; and the said Bailiff and Commonalty shall contribute with the Barons to do service touching ships for the fleet, and no one of the said member shall plead or be impleaded before the King or elsewhere touching matters arising in the said member save in the bailiff's court or in the Court of the Cinque Ports called 'Shepewaia', as the Barons of the Ports are commissioned to plead'.

Thus the town of Tenterden and the shipbuilding communities of Smallhythe and Reading within the Hundred of Tenterden were incorporated by royal charter with Rye, one of the head ports of the Cinque Ports Confederation, as a member or 'limb', to help her maintain the quota of ships required of her by the Confederation. Rye's

to demolish his chief residence - there is no record of such drastic action having to be taken. The fine for refusal had risen to £40 by the 18th century. Corporate income was derived mainly from the town scot and the letting of the fair, and to a lesser degree from town rents and fines. As the most spacious and commodious building in the locality, St Mildred's Church may well have been used by the Tenterden Corporation in its early days for the conduct of official business. The first known reference to a Court Hall does not occur until 1509, some 60 years after the Charter. The original Court Hall, and gaol, probably stood in the area at the top of what is now Station Road where the Fire Station stood until 1971. It was burnt down in 1660 by an inmate of the gaol; he escaped, but many of the old records of the town were destroyed. The first Bailiff elected in 1449 was Thomas Pittlesden, whose personal coat of arms is shown on the mizzen mast of the ship illustrated on the town's coat of arms (the coat of arms on the main mast is that of the Cinque Ports Confederation). An amended charter granted by Elizabeth I in 1600 maintained all the rights and conditions laid down in 1449, but the office of Bailiff was changed to that of Mayor. The granting of the Charter not only changed the administration of the Town and Hundred in the 15th century, but as we shall see in later chapters, it also affected decisions made in the centuries to come.

CHAPTER TWO

1449 to 1837

THERE WERE other benefits from the wealth generated locally in the 15th century, which was referred to in the previous chapter. These were the erection of the fine tower of St Mildred's (above), which still today dominates that part of the High Street, and is an easily discernible landmark from all points of the compass, and the later opening of a grammar school. The church tower was started in 1465, financed by funds accruing from benefactors

the tower is a double west door, a surprising and unusual feature for an ordinary parish church. In fact, there are only six churches in England which have double doors like this, and two of them are in Kent - the other is at Lydd.

The Grammar School was housed in a building started in 1485, now a shop occupied by Viyella (see page 34). Its foundation in the early 16th century is attributed to 'an ancestor of the family of Heyman of Somerfield', who 'founded the free school in this town for teaching the Latin tongue gratis to so many poor children of this parish as the Mayor and Jurats should think proper who are the trustees of it and appoint the Master, but at present there are no children on this foundation. William Marshall, clerk, about the year 1521 gave £10 per annum to be paid to the Master of the school out of a messuage and 12 acres of land in this parish'. This statement is from Hasted, writing in the late 18th century; he was used to being governed by a Mayor, and failed to realise that the town was run by a Bailiff prior to 1600. Other bequests followed, including 10s from George Strekenbold in 1525 and 13s 4d from George ffelype in 1551. Despite Hasted's statement that the Mayor and Jurats were trustees of the school, it would appear that the church authorities were the supreme directors of its day-to-day running and welfare. Several Archdeacons' Visitations would seem to confirm this.

For instance, in 1559 the churchwardens were told to 'enquire of the state of the Schoole and to certyficate whether they come to church, behave themselves well and decentlie

and other gifts. The stone used was called Bethersden marble, which was rough hewn and quarried at Tuesnoad near the village. If one examines the structure today, small shells may be seen in the stone. Incorporated in

theare or no'; in 1560 'they have a skolemaster that doth teach grammar but what grammar they know not'; and in 1576 there was 'William Harris who teacheth grammar in our town and one Henry Robinson who teacheth English within our parish, but whether either of them is licensed is not known'.

Further confirmation of the church's involvement could come from the names of the succession of schoolmasters recorded as teaching at the school, including George Ely, Vicar of Tenterden 1571-1615, and various chaplains of Smallhythe. Also, according to a later document entitled 'Catalogue of Promocons etc in ye Diocese of Canterbury 1663', 'Tenterden Free Schoole belongs to ye gift of ye Vicar'. In 1702 came perhaps the biggest bequest of the lot when John Mantell gave £200 to the school to be laid out to purchase 10 acres of land at St Mary-in-the-Marsh, let at £10 per annum to be paid to the Master of the school. The following year, however, when the master was Humphrey Hammond MA, the chaplain of Smallhythe, the school became embroiled in a lengthy lawsuit. An attempt was made to recover an annuity of 40s due to the church which had not been paid since 1685, and the annuity of £10 referred to earlier which had been refused. Sir John Hales as inheritor of the lands involved was accused of not honouring his obligations, and after two years of complex investigation, it was decreed that 'the said Humphrey Hammond (should receive) the sum of seventeen pounds ten shillings due and unpaid from Christmas 1703 and also that certain lands containing by estimation

THE OLD GRAMMAR SCHOOL 1903 51002

12 acres lying in Tenterden be charged with ten pounds to the Schoolmaster of the free schoole of Tenterden for the time beinge'. Thus the financial security of the school was settled; but by the end of the century, the number of pupils had declined (as per Hasted earlier in this chapter), and eventually the school closed in 1817.

In 1533 King Henry VIII broke from Rome and established himself as head of the Church of England, suppressing the monasteries. St Mildred's Church, in line with this decision, was withdrawn from the patronage of the Abbot of St Augustine's and came under the control of the Dean and Chapter of Canterbury Cathedral. In 1534, Thomas Cromwell was appointed the King's Chief Minister, and the Act of Supremacy was passed in December of that year. This Act secured the ecclesiastical supremacy to the Crown and excluded the authority of the Pope. After Henry's death, the church entered difficult times; the chaos which followed is evidenced by the number of clergy, both nationally and in relation to Tenterden itself, who came and went in a short space of time. One was the Rev Bostock, curate of St Mildred's, who was committed to Newgate Prison for preaching a seditious sermon. Like most communities in England, the Weald had its share of religious martyrs. During the reign of Mary, several Protestants were burnt at the stake in Wincheap, Canterbury, having been held in the north porch of St Mildred's the night before. Under Elizabeth I, Catholicism was

Tenterden Families Emigrating to New England

In April 1635, the families of Nathaniel Tilden, Samuel Hinckley, Jonas Austen and John Lewis, along with others from the Weald, sailed from Sandwich in the ship 'Hercules'. The voyage to New England lasted nearly three months, and landfall was eventually made near Plymouth on its coast. Most of the emigrants settled just to the south, beside an area with a natural harbour and several streams supplying water, later to become the town of Scituate. Tilden and Hinckley remained there, but little is known of where or how Austen and Lewis prospered. Nathaniel Tilden, who had been to New England before and had acquired property there, became a prominent citizen (he was an Elder of the First Church), but he died in 1641. His sons all prospered in their new country, and founded a family whose descendants now live in many states of the USA and are frequent visitors to Tenterden. His most famous descendant is undoubtedly Samuel Tilden, Governor of New York, who lost the Presidency in 1865 after a suspect recount. There is a 'Tilden corner' in the Town Museum. Samuel Hinckley later moved to Barnstable near Cape Cod, where his eldest son became Governor of Plymouth Colony.

gradually deemed unlawful, and it remained so for over 300 years. St Mildred's therefore began its history of congregations in the Church of England: services were conducted in the English language, and the Bible, also translated into English, stood in pride of place for all those who could read.

But as the town entered the 17th century, the first seeds of nonconformity were being sown; these were to be nurtured over the centuries to result in the present count of three Anglican, one Catholic and five nonconformist churches in Tenterden today. For a considerable time, many parishioners had been presented at the time of the Archdeacon's Visitations for non-attendance at church on Sundays, and in particular for not taking Communion. Some of those mentioned were the wife of Henry Merriott, who was presented for her 'usuall neglect of cominge to divine service and for not receiving Communion at Easter last nor since, and beinge by mee admonished thereof and advised to conforme herselfe to the orders of the church', and George Wright and Thomas Wybourn, who were 'late or negligent comers to church upon Sundayes and holidays to Morning and Evening prayer'.

This state of affairs might also have contributed to the desire of Tenterden people to emigrate to New England. The main voyage was that made by a party of Wealden families, including four from Tenterden, in the ship 'Hercules' in 1635. Although they were regarded by some as dissenters, they nevertheless had to be endorsed by the Vicar of Tenterden before being allowed to sail. Most of the Tenterden families settled at the coastal town of Scituate in what was later to become Massachusetts, and generally prospered in their new land. Emigration to New England occurred largely between 1620 and 1650; many immigrants died in their first year because of the intense cold and hunger following the privations of a ten-week voyage in a ship of only 200 tons.

During the Cromwellian period in the middle of the 17th century, Tenterden saw little of the fighting except for a few local skirmishes. Soldiers were billeted at Little Westwell in the Rolvenden Road where their billeting numbers can still be seen today. However, all weddings conducted during Commonwealth times were not before the Vicar, but instead were taken by a local Jurat. The Rev George Hawe had been appointed as Vicar of Tenterden by Cromwell, but when the Restoration of the monarch occurred in 1662, he refused to adhere to the Act of Uniformity and to renounce the Solemn League and Covenant of 1643, and was thrown out of the living. He decided to arrange services along Presbyterian lines for a considerable number of adherents, and set up what was to become the Unitarian Church (page 38), the first nonconformist one in Tenterden.

For many years this new set of worshippers met in local houses, and it was not until 1748 that the Old Meeting House was erected as their church in the Ashford Road. Other nonconformist churches were to follow towards the end of the 18th century,

THE UNITARIAN CHURCH 2004   T24714k (Alan Brand)

starting with a chapel in Honey Lane (now Bells Lane). From these roots grew the Baptist church, which was to split in the 19th century into the Zion Baptists, whose church stands at the end of Bridewell Lane, and the Jireh Strict Baptists, whose chapel is at St Michaels. The Wesleyan Methodist church also had its beginning in Honey Lane, but the present church at West Cross dates only from 1885. A much later church, the Trinity Baptist on the corner of Turners Avenue, has been in existence for just over 30 years.

Although they were not directly affected by the ecclesiastical discord of the Cromwellian period, the town's inns were in their heyday in the 17th century. The three

Did you know?

The Eight Bells

This public house was originally called the Angel, and tokens with angels on them (similar to those issued for the Tenterden Brewery) could be honoured on the premises. In the 1730s, the name was changed to the Six Bells because of its proximity to St Mildred's Church. In 1770, when the church peal was increased, it became the Eight Bells which we know today.

THE WHITE LION 2004 T24709k (Alan Brand)

THE EIGHT BELLS 2004 T2471 0k (Alan Brand)

oldest establishments which still exist today, the Woolpack (44994), the Eight Bells (T24710k) and the White Lion (51001 and T24709k), all started as hall houses in the 15th century, and were converted in line with most other buildings of this nature in the following century when they became inns.

HIGH STREET, THE WOOLPACK INN 1900   44994t

THE WHITE LION 1903 51001

It is considered that the vast spaces of St Mildred's Church were used for public occasions as well as ecclesiastical ones, but these three inns were undoubtedly centres of town life at that time. The town had been without a civic centre from 1661, when the Court Hall was burnt down, and an extension which had been added to the Woolpack in the 18th century, including an assembly room and a card room, was incorporated into the new Town Hall of 1790 next door. The card room became the present Mayor's Parlour. Two other public houses still in existence today are the William Caxton and the Vine, both dating from circa 1800, although some of the former is thought to be earlier. The name of the William Caxton dates only from 1951; before that date it had been called the Black Horse – it was renamed as part of Tenterden's celebrations for the Festival of Britain. The two public houses in St Michaels, the Crown and the Fat Ox, are later buildings.

THE VINE INN c1950 T24017a

There are older pubs of varying dates which are now in use as different businesses. These include the New Inn. Originally part of a 15th-century hall house and extensively altered 100 years later, it became a beer house in the 19th century. At one time it was called This Ancient Borough, but it closed as an inn after 1945 and is now the Honeymoon Chinese Restaurant. The Harris Arms is part of a replacement of earlier buildings on the site of what is now 9-15 High Street; it became the Harris Arms in the early 1800s. It was closed 100 years later, and the premises were used as a variety of small shops. Now 9-11 is the local Woolworth's, and the remainder is Cafe Uno. The Queens Arms opened in the

THE NEW INN c1950 T24009

THE WILLIAM CAXTON C1955 T24047

17th century; the premises were part of three buildings which had replaced an earlier hall house. It was refaced with mathematical tiles in the late 18th century, and it closed in the 20th century. Its exact location on the south side of the High Street is not known.

Ye Olde Cellars started life in 1700 as cellars for Avery's, the wine merchants; the family retained the business for nearly 200 years. In the 1880s, the drinking saloon was opened in its underground site. A favourite 'watering hole', it closed in 1986 and is now occupied by Boardroom. The Plough, situated at the end of Golden Square, was originally a 16th-century barn, and was converted to an ale house in 1762. It is now a private house, aptly named Plough Cottage. Little is recorded of

the George's history, but the building is now the estate agents Your Move. The Gardeners Arms was a popular pub in the 20th century, but it was closed post-War. Recently occupied by Garden Antiques, it is now called Quill House.

The White Hart Inn, Reading Street, appeared in the records for 1659, but it dates probably from earlier times, as the white hart, the badge of Richard II, was one of the earliest names adopted for inn signs. Rebuilt in 1900, it was renamed the White Hart and Lamb, but it closed in the 1960s to become a private residence. As for the Greyhound, nothing is known of its history or its exact location.

On the western side of what is now Coombe

THE WILLIAM CAXTON 2004   T24711k (Alan Brand)

Lane was a piece of land known as Timson's Gardens. The plot was purchased in 1792 by Isaac Cloake, a brewer and member of the Ebony family of graziers, who with his brother Thankful set up a brewery at the rear. To live in, they had a new double-fronted house built between the brewery and the High Street, which today is that part at the rear of the Vine Inn. In 1796, during a time of a national shortage of copper coins, the Cloakes issued a trade token, the Tenterden Halfpenny, which could be used to purchase drink at the brewery. The token bore the arms of the Brewers Society on the face; on the reverse side were a horse and dray loaded with barrels and an inscription, 'to cheer our hearts'; and round the rim were the words 'payable at I & T Cloake's Brewhouse'.

Did you know?

Tenterden Brewery

The brewery started by Isaac and Thankful Cloake in 1792 was bought after Isaac's death by Samuel Shepherd, the Faversham brewer and founder of what was to become Shepherd Neame. Eventually it was owned by a Tenterden family, Obadiah Edwards and his sons. The brewery closed in the early 20th century; during the 1950s, the building was used by Kent Chemical Company. The building was then demolished, and the area is now used as a coach park. Station Road was originally called Brewhouse Lane.

TENTERDEN, HIGH STREET c1950 T24007t

BOROUGH PLACE 2004 T24702k (Alan Brand)

In earlier centuries, the lot of the poor had been particularly hard, living in hovels and often starving. However, the Poor Law Act of 1601 had legislated for poor people to receive organised relief under the jurisdiction of local overseers, who were appointed to collect the local poor rate levied on those who could pay, and then to distribute the funds to the needy. Although hardships and abuses existed, there is much evidence that the poor were reasonably well cared for by weekly payments of money, payment of rents, and provision of clothes, fuel, medical attention, and apprenticeships for children. This evidence can be found in the Accounts of the Overseers of the Poor of Tenterden, where local tradesmen are cited as supplying

food, footwear, and so on. A poor house, built in Elizabethan times where Borough Place now stands, was maintained for those in need of accommodation; it was enlarged in the early 18th century.

In contrast to the attention that had been paid to the poor in the town, the 18th century saw provision being made for the more affluent at the time of their retirement. In 1768, an Annuity Society was formed whereby for a quarterly payment of 5s, a member qualified for a pension of £8 per annum at the age of 60, provided that he had paid in for at least 20 years. A widow of a member was entitled to such payment immediately after her husband's death and for the rest of her life, providing she did not remarry. Should she bear a child after one year or more of widowhood, she no longer qualified for a pension! Other conditions were formulated both at the outset and in later years in light of experience gained. The main ones were firstly, that the quarterly payment had to be made in person to the Society's Treasurer at the prescribed meeting place; in practice, the 3 main pubs took it in turns to host the meeting. Secondly, any default in payment was penalized by way of a fine, and after three missed payments the member was struck off and no monies made available to him. The Society was lenient with those who were justifiably sick. Thirdly, an age limit of 40 and over was imposed for wives of older members to stop the latter marrying young ladies who could become widows for many years! To administer the Society, three members were appointed for any given year as Directors responsible for its solvency; any refusal resulted in a heavy fine. From the Society's start in 1768, membership rose steadily; by the early 19th century, pensions well above the £8 figure were being paid out. But later on in the century, membership declined, and extra payments had to sought to allow the pensions to be honoured. Lloyd George's provision for old age pension in Edwardian times led to the Society being wound up after World War I.

Somewhere in between the rich and the poor were the tradesmen of the town, although the wealthier ones were probably Annuity Society members. The trades varied from blacksmiths to glove makers, boot makers, and carpenters, and to the precision world of watch makers, clock makers and gunsmiths. Two families of blacksmiths existed for several centuries cheek by jowl at West Cross: Beale's was on the present site of the Indian restaurant, and Milsted's where the houses stand on the corner of West Cross Gardens. The Beale family made edged tools, and were famous for the Tenterden billhook designed and made by Thomas Beale, one of

The Curteis Family

One of the prominent Tenterden families during this period was the Curteis family. William Curteis had come to the town in 1572 from the Romney Marsh area, where he already held lands. His descendants gradually acquired land and property in many of the villages surrounding Tenterden as well as in the town itself. Perhaps the most successful of these was Jeremiah Curteis, Mayor of Tenterden on three occasions, who set about acquiring much of the old Heronden land; by the 19th century, virtually all the south-west part of the parish west of the Smallhythe Road was Curteis property. Later on, Curteis ladies married into the Pomfret and Croughton families, whose members played a major part in the town's affairs during that century. There were wealthy branches of the Curteis family in other parts of Kent, and also in Sussex, where many commemorative plaques may be seen in Wartling church.

41 designs nationwide. Milsted's undertook more traditional smithying and farrier work. In the late 19th century, Milsted's bought out Beale's and ran both businesses until its closure in 1954. There was also a dye works and tannery later on in the West Cross area, and one can imagine the smoke, smell and noise when these places were in full operation. Records show that clockmakers were in the town at least from 1750; such names as William Hopkins, Wraight and Woolley were well-known throughout Kent. Watchmakers were also prominent, such as Owen Jackson in what is now Webb's ironmongers (note Jacksons Lane alongside the premises) and John Masters (see the shield on Jumpers shop inscribed 'JM 1858'). Masters had taken over from William Birch, who started business in the late 18th century.

RYE ROAD 1901 46367

This road is now called Smallhythe Road.

Windmills and Watermills

During the 19th century, cereal growing in the land around Tenterden was sufficiently intense to require nine mills for grinding the corn. Windmills were in use at Leigh Green, Mill Lane, Ashbourne, Goodshill Shoreham Lane, and Glebe Field, but all had ceased operation by the early 20th century. A set of three watermills also flourished during the same period; the first one at the Millponds (on the Roman Road from Benenden)

THE MILL POND 1901 46371

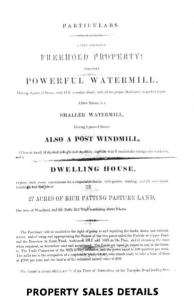

ASHBOURNE MILL 2004 T24703k (Alan Brand)

PARTICULARS.

A VERY DESIRABLE

FREEHOLD PROPERTY!

Comprising a

POWERFUL WATERMILL,

Driving 3 pairs of Stones, with 18 ft. overshot wheel, with all the proper Machinery in perfect repair

Above Stream is a

SMALLER WATERMILL,

Driving 2 pairs of Stones

ALSO A POST WINDMILL,

(Close at hand) of superior strength and capability, together with 6 comfortable cottages for workmen,
and a

DWELLING HOUSE,

replete with every convenience for a respectable family, with garden, stabling, and all convenient
buildings, and throughout

27 ACRES OF RICH FATTING PASTURE LAND,

One acre of Woodland, and the Table Mill Pond containing about 9 acres.

**PROPERTY SALES DETAILS
1851** ZZZ00232
(Reproduced by kind permission of the
Tenterden Local History Society)

was supplied with water from the nearby Breeches Pond, so named because of its shape (46371). The excess water from the mill, boosted by other millponds and streams, was then used to drive the second mill at the bottom of Goodshill on the Cranbrook Road. Here again, water flowed on from this site, and strengthened by additional streams, turned the wheel at Ashbourne Mill (T24703k), the non-working building still standing near Rolvenden Station

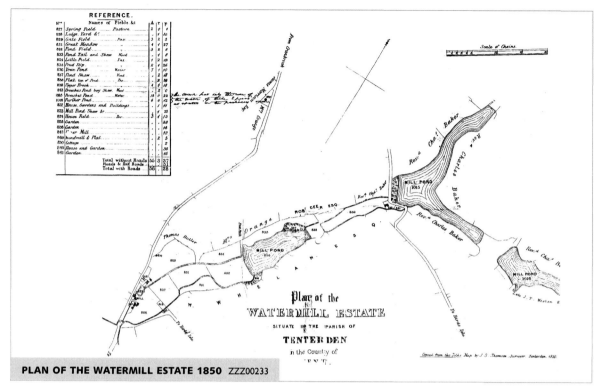

PLAN OF THE WATERMILL ESTATE 1850 ZZZ00233

(Reproduced by kind permission of the Tenterden Local History Society)

Beyond the town centre, agriculture was the main occupation of landowners and workers. The area was mainly used for grazing sheep, although there were some cattle farmers and graziers, who were also butchers. Unlike in Tenterden's very early days, there seems to have been very little pig farming. On the more productive soil south of the town, farmers grew cereal crops, and there were orchards of apples, pears and cherries (see T24019).

But the predominant crop was hops, which generated wealth not only for the farmers but also seasonal income for local families. In the springtime, local women were employed to 'twiddle' the hop bines up poles; but when 'wire fields' were introduced, they did the same thing up strings which had been suspended from hooks on the overhead wire system. Then in September every year, the womenfolk and their families spent the whole month picking the fully grown hops into sacking 'bins' to earn money for clothing their children. Two or three times a day the amount of hops picked into each bin was measured by a 'measurer' with a wicker basket; the pickers were originally given metal 'tallies' recording the amount picked, but later the same information was written into a record book. The picked hops were placed in 'pokes', sacks which held 10 bushels, and were then taken to oast houses for drying and eventual pressing into long 'pockets', which weighed

A TYPICAL KENT ORCHARD COTTAGE AND OAST HOUSE C1955 T24019

one and a quarter hundredweight when full. The pockets were conveyed to hop warehouses near London Bridge, later reflected in the old telephone code of HOP for that area.

In 1835, an event occurred which set the scene for Victorian Tenterden, as we shall see in the next chapter.

**QUEEN ELIZABETH'S CHARTER,
THE TENTERDEN TAPESTRY**
ZZZ00241

**SHIPBUILDING AT SMALL HYTHE,
THE TENTERDEN TAPESTRY**
ZZZ00240

(Reproduced by kind permission of the Tenterden Museum)

CHAPTER THREE

The Victorian Era

VICTORIA came to the throne in 1837, a young princess after a succession of older kings. Similarly, local government in Tenterden was in the hands of a new type of body, Tenterden Borough Council, set up following the introduction of the Municipal Corporations Act of 1835. The Act swept away the old forms of local government and instituted representative councils with properly appointed officers, elected on a wider franchise and subject to regular critical scrutiny. These bodies were more fitted to tackle efficiently the manifold civic problems of the day. Thus in 1836 a new council took office, consisting of 12 councillors who chose from their number a Mayor and four Aldermen. On petition, a Commission of Peace was granted and a Recorder appointed to hold the Court of Quarter Sessions. Although under the Act the new council's functions were somewhat limited, it was empowered to draft bye-laws, collect rates and organise an efficient police force – this had been formed soon after 1835. Later in the era, after a fire had destroyed the roof of the Town Hall in 1879, the new Corporation took over the control of the town's fire engines. In 1896, the brigade ceased to be a voluntary organisation and came under the direct control of the Corporation (Borough of Tenterden) Fire Brigade.

Did you know?

Tenterden Borough Police

Nowadays, Tenterden has no police force stationed in the town; but in 1836 the new Borough Council very quickly organised one. It consisted of a High Constable, three constables, and a number of watchmen who were in effect night constables – they were given refreshments at the Black Horse during their duty. The force was supplemented as and when required by special constables. One of their duties was to ensure that the public houses and inns were closed on time on Saturday nights and Sundays. They were eventually amalgamated with the Kent County Constabulary.

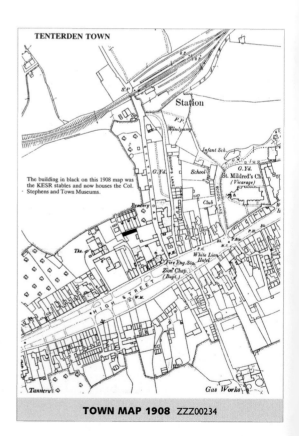

TENTERDEN TOWN

The building in black on this 1908 map was the KESR stables and now houses the Col. Stephens and Town Museums.

TOWN MAP 1908 ZZZ00234

THE BOROUGH OF TENTERDEN FIRE ENGINE ZZZ00007

(Reproduced by kind permission of the Tenterden Local History Society)

Life in the town, and in particular the surrounding countryside, did not necessarily reflect this new feeling of achievement. Agriculture had been in decline since the start of the century, when the introduction of machinery onto the farms had led to a reduced number of agricultural labourers being required. Some of these men resorted to violent action by burning buildings and stacks, the so-called Swing Riots. Jobs became scarce, and many families had to throw themselves on the mercy of charitable organisations. For instance, as the situation continued to worsen during the era, a soup kitchen was set up in 1875 in Jacksons Lane.

THE SOUP KITCHEN IN JACKSON'S LANE 2004
T24704k (Alan Brand)

ZION BAPTIST CHURCH 1902 49076

The poverty of the time doubtless led to some men stealing food and other items needed by their families, resulting in even more cases of transportation to Australia. Many others were forced to declare themselves paupers and be committed to the workhouse. Originally the old poor house (Borough Place) had been used, but it was much too small at this time; the Board of Guardians therefore decided to have a new and larger one built at the west end of the town. (This building is now West View Hospital, soon to be demolished and newer hospital premises erected nearby). The land was obtained in 1843, and the workhouse opened in 1846. The workhouse, built to hold 450 persons, provided a minimum subsistence under conditions which were deliberately designed to deter all but the utterly desperate. It was intended to be as unpleasant as possible; for instance, married couples were separated, and children were taken from their parents. None could leave the premises except on special occasions, and visits were limited to once a week. Life was probably as grim as Dickens described in 'Oliver Twist', and more locally by Dorothy Hatcher in 'The Workhouse and the Weald'. Hard manual labour was meted out to the sturdier inmates, particularly any vagrant committed to the workhouse by the police. By 1930, the building had ceased to be a workhouse; it was used initially as a hospital for mentally defective women, and then post-1945 as a geriatric hospital.

Despite the gloom arising from the decline in agriculture in the countryside, life in the town itself was on a better footing. In 1843, as a result of a meeting backed by the new council, but arranged and supported by the townspeople as a whole, it was agreed that the streets in the town should be lit by gas. A local rate was assessed, sufficient to pay for the necessary lamps and the gas works to provide the fuel for the lighting. The works were built at the end of what is at present called Bridewell Lane, and a manager and staff were appointed to run it. The lane was at that time called Chapel Lane in recognition of the church at its High Street end, now known as the Zion Baptist Church (49076 page 58). Efforts were made to rename it Gas Lane, but the old name was retained in people's memories; for instance, the 1851 Census enumerator for that part of the town chose to use Chapel Lane for his returns. However, the name of

Gas Lane was eventually accepted, and as older inhabitants of the town will remember, this name endured well into the 20th century until the gas company was closed down.

The early Victorian times also saw a bitter and lengthy period of litigation between the local landowners and the Vicar of Tenterden, Philip Ward, who had taken up his appointment in 1830, coming to the town with his wife and five children. His wife, Horatia, was none other than the illegitimate daughter of Lord Nelson and Lady Hamilton (who was the wife of the Ambassador at Naples). The vicarage in 1830 was in a generally poor state, and certainly unfit to house a young couple and a growing family, so the Wards lived in other accommodation near the White Lion for two years whilst the vicarage was rebuilt. Horatia had five more children during her lifetime in Tenterden, two of whom died in infancy.

Perhaps because of the expense of looking after this increasing family, Philip Ward attempted to have his portion of the tithes

Mrs Horatia Ward

Horatia was born in 1801, the daughter of Lord Nelson and Emma Lady Hamilton. After rather a lonely childhood, and without her father (he was killed at Trafalgar in 1805), she met Philip Ward at Burnham in Norfolk in 1819. She had been rather fond of the Rev Blake, the curate of that parish, but when Philip Ward succeeded him in the post, the allegedly handsome newcomer won her heart. They married in 1822; the ceremony was conducted by the Rev William Bolton, Horatia's uncle. Philip had curacies at various Norfolk parishes before obtaining the position of Vicar of Tenterden, where Horatia spent many happy years. When Philip died in 1859, Horatia was required to vacate the vicarage, and she moved to Pinner in Middlesex to live with her second oldest son Nelson Ward, Registrar in the Chancery Court. She was awarded a pension of £300 per annum by Queen Victoria, but in 1881 she died at Pinner and was buried there in the Paines Lane Cemetery.

due to him raised to what he considered to be a reasonable level. Prior to 1836, the situation regarding tithes had been rather difficult to understand. After centuries of tithes being rendered 'in kind' (hence the tithe barns around the countryside), there was in the 1830s a mixture of entirely in kind, of monetary payments in lieu, and a 'some and some' compromise. By an Act in 1836, it was laid down that in future all tithes should be in the form of money only, which necessitated a full-scale assessment being made in every parish throughout the country. Philip Ward was not satisfied with his allocation of £200 per annum (this was the lesser vicarial tithe due to him - the greater rectorial tithes were granted to the Dean and Chapter of Canterbury). After litigation which lasted 10 years, he succeeded in his aim; but the landowners, led by Thomas Buss Shoobridge, appealed against the decision. The appeal was heard in front of the Lord Chief Justice, with the landowners' case put by the Solicitor-General. But after it had been demonstrated that the agent retained by the landowners had deliberately down-rated the tithe assessment field by field, the case collapsed, and Philip Ward won the day. He was awarded an annual sum of £450, plus £2600 arrears for the ten years of the disputed case. The litigation had cost the landowners £6600 overall, but it is not known how much Rev Ward had to pay.

Furley, the 19th-century Kent historian, alleged that there was a lot of ill-will generated by this court action, but perhaps that lasted only a short time; for upon Philip's death in

ST MILDRED'S CHURCH 1903 51004

1859, the parishioners erected a stained glass window in his memory at the end of the north aisle in St Mildred's.

In 1930, the Bishop of Dover, when visiting the church to plan for this area to be converted into a Lady Chapel, objected to the subject depicted in the window (Christ's temptation by the Devil), and ordered a replacement one. The original window was transported to Woodton Church in Norfolk, where it was re-erected. Woodton was where Lord Nelson's mother had been born - her father was the local rector. Thus in a rather roundabout manner, the Nelson connection was maintained.

The Victorian era was nationally the time of great development in the provision of railways. Various projects were put forward to include Tenterden in the network, but all of them failed, mainly because of the lack of finance. The one which seemed most likely to succeed, from Paddock Wood to Hythe, was started late in the 19th century, but was terminated at Hawkhurst; even that one, however, would not have touched the town centre, but instead would have gone to the west of Tenterden. Nevertheless, the coming of the South Eastern Railway from London to Dover through Tonbridge and Ashford did have an influence on that other form of transport, the horse-drawn coach. The building of the turnpike road from Cranbrook to Romney in 1762 had affected the scope of this form of transport in improving its operation. The turnpike and other subsidiary roads were paid for both in construction and maintenance by tolls collected at toll houses and toll gates, situated for example at Castweazle on the Rolvenden Road and Cherry Gardens on the Woodchurch Road, as well as in the High Street near St Mildred's (44993c).

THE OLD TOLL HOUSE AND THE JAIL 1900 44993c

GOLDEN SQUARE c1960 T24073

The freight waggon, which had taken three days each way in its journey to and from London, could now operate on a twice-weekly basis. By 1839 the coaches for passengers were the Tally Ho coach, which left the Woolpack daily except Sundays at 6.45am for London via Headcorn and Maidstone; and the Flower of Kent coach, which left the Woolpack at 6.15am three days per week for London via Cranbrook and Tonbridge.

The coming of the railways a few years later was instrumental in closing down these direct coaching journeys, but the operators of the horse-drawn vehicles quickly revised their routes to compensate. A good example of this was R & J Bennett & Co of Bennett's Yard. This firm had been founded in c1800 as hauliers and coal merchants, but by the 1850s they were able to offer the following services with their omnibuses: daily to and from Headcorn for the London trains, daily to and from Maidstone for the North Kent trains, daily to and from Rye for the Hastings trains, and twice weekly to and from Hawkhurst,

with parcels deliveries daily to Rolvenden and the neighbourhood. Other operators offered services to and from Appledore, Cranbrook and Ashford.

The British Empire is usually regarded as being at its height during Queen Victoria's reign, and the exploits of the British Army are similarly to the fore at that time. There is, however, surprisingly little in Tenterden's history about military exploits. The century had started with the Napoleonic wars still unfinished and the threat of an invasion by the French; the building of the Royal Military Canal from Hythe to Rye was one of the main defences against such an eventuality. Regular soldiers were based at barracks near Reading Street (Barracks Farm still stands in that area), and the officers from there were the main supporters of the small theatre in Bells Lane; note the existence still of Theatre Square and the nearby Theatre Cottages.

In addition to the regulars and the militia who were called to the colours, Tenterden supplied several units of the Cinque Ports

Bennett's Yard

The yard of R & J Bennett & Co was situated where Bennetts Mews are today. The firm started in the early 1800s: the Pictorial Record in December 1899 recorded that 'R & J Bennett & Co, omnibus proprietors and general carriers, also coal and coke merchants, has existed for nearly a century. Founder was W Bennett, grandfather of the younger partners. The firm has branch stabling at Headcorn and Biddenden, and a farm at London Beach where a good proportion of the forage is grown for their 40 horses. Landaus, waggonettes, pleasure brakes, omnibuses, cob chaises and carts for hire. Horse buses run between Tenterden, Maidstone, Headcorn, Rye and Hawkhurst, and from Tenterden to London. Agents for the South Eastern & Chatham Railway'. The firm converted to petrol buses in the early part of the 20th century, when buses from rival companies also used the yard to stable overnight.

TO THE THEATRE SQUARE 2004 T24705k (Alan Brand)

Volunteers, who would have supplemented the other defence forces in the event of an invasion. But through the remainder of the century there is no mention of military affairs until its very end: the Crimean War and the various campaigns on the African continent are not mentioned, but right at the end of the era, there are reports of Tenterden men joining the East Kent Regiment (the Buffs) to fight against the Boers. One man who features prominently is Vivian Dampier-Palmer, who later became a leading citizen of the town. After service in the Coldstream Guards, he was sent to South Africa in 1899 as a Second Lieutenant in the Buffs. He was involved in much of the bitter fighting, and ended the war as a Captain. Other soldiers who served in that campaign were given a civic reception upon their return to this country.

THE 5TH BUFFS 1911 ZZZ00165

(Reproduced by kind permission of Tenterden Local History Society)

THE NATIONAL SCHOOL 2004 T24706k (Alan Brand)

Following the demise of the Grammar School (see the previous chapter), free education for the town's children depended initially on the National School, which opened in 1843 in what was then known as School Lane (above). It had taken over from the Grammar School, and is usually associated with St Mildred's Church nearby. In 1845, to cater for children from nonconformist families, a British School was set up in the Ashford Road. Both these schools continued to have pupils the whole length of the century, and in fact well into the 20th century. In 1957, the British School closed, and the 8–11-year-olds from both that school and the National School were transferred to a new Junior School in Recreation Ground Road. The National School continued as an infants-only establishment until 1973, when it moved to a new separate building in Recreation Ground Road. Later in the 19th century, there was a National School in Smallhythe at the top of Summer Hill, which is no longer there. In 1865, a further National School was started in St Michael's, of which more later.

For those parents able and willing to pay for their children's education, there were private schools also available in the town. As early as 1764, a Mr Buckland had advertised his school; for a time it had catered also for some of the pupils in the Grammar School during its declining years, until he moved to Sutton Valence. At about the same time, Stephen and Sarah Dewar opened a girls' boarding school 'at the very easy price of Half a Guinea Entrance and Twelve Guineas per year'.

By 1792, a boys' day school was functioning at Clare House (T24707k, now Westbourne), and Pigot's Directory of 1812 mentions two ladies' schools, Sarah Blundell's and the Misses Hodges', and two boys' day schools, William Guy's and John Rofe's. Stephen Rofe opened a day school at the present 112 High Street; Henry Lansdell opened a day and boarding school at the Manor House; and Sarah Wafter opened a day school and Sarah Mills a boarding school, both at East Cross. In 1838, a schoolroom was added to the Unitarian minister's house, and a Mr Taylor ran a school there which later continued throughout the remainder of the century. From 1893, the Limes High School for Girls functioned with Miss Woods as Principal. The curriculum claimed a thorough education in English and foreign languages, music, art, callisthenics and dancing, with the girls being prepared for the Cambridge Locals and other examinations.

CLARE HOUSE 2004 T24707k (Alan Brand)

EAST CROSS GARDENS c1955 T24039

Mathematical Tiles

Mathematical tiles, also known as brick tiles, are hanging tiles designed to simulate bricks. The dictionary definition of 'mathematical is 'rigorously precise', and perhaps the tiles' name comes from the need for precision in the shaping of both their front and rear surfaces. Out of Kent's total of 300 buildings which used these tiles, Tenterden had 32. The tiles were introduced in the late 18th century, but carried on into the next century. Their original use was to give a modern appearance to timber-framed buildings, but later they were used from the outset to look like bricks on new buildings. There are examples in Tenterden on either side of the High Street, and include the White Lion and Laura Ashley's. Others outside the town centre include The Cedars in Smallhythe Road and Dovenden in Woodchurch Road. In such cases, red tiles were used, as in buildings at Hythe and Canterbury; those in Ashford are buff-coloured.

The 19th century saw real growth in the nonconformist churches – by 1900 they numbered four in all. From the 18th-century chapel in Honey Lane sprang both the Baptist church and the Methodist church. What is now the Zion Baptist Church was built in 1835 when it was obvious that the church had a rapidly increasing membership, too great for the old chapel. It was rebuilt in 1887 – the date is shown on the front of the building. Members were prominent in many ways during the ensuing years; for instance, in 1846 four members served on the committee of the British School. In 1864, members were leading figures in the Tenterden Benevolent Society, an institution for the relief of the sick. Some years later, the Baptists were associated with other Christian organisations in the founding of a Social Welfare Association for Tenterden and the surrounding district. Back in 1841, some people had become dissatisfied with the General Baptist ministry, and established a Strict Baptist church. Several different

venues were used over the years, and in the 1860s the current chapel in Grange Road appeared to be insufficient for the members' requirements. Through the auspices of a donor of land and various other gifts, the present chapel in the Ashford Road was built in 1869. As for the Methodist church, the land on which the present church stands was purchased as early as 1796 with the intention of building a place of worship for Methodists. Although there are records of Methodist churches in the district, for instance at Rolvenden, and High Halden, it was only in 1885 that a permanent church was constructed (51003, page 71).

Several other important alterations and additions took place in ecclesiastical establishments in the town during Victorian times. At St Mildred's in 1864, extensive restoration work was undertaken when Philip Ward's successor, the Rev Mereweather, was Vicar. He oversaw the removal of the galleries and the box pews, and the chancel arch was widened and repairs made to the window

TENTERDEN, WESLEYAN CHAPEL 1903 51003

tracery (45002). Later, in 1899, Mr James Dampier-Palmer presented the church with the choir stalls and screen, the chancel screen and a new lectern and pulpit.

In 1867, during the time of the Roman Catholic revival in the 19th century, the Benedictine fathers of an Anglo-Belgian congregation from Ramsgate established a priory at Finchden on the Appledore Road (page 72). This was the first known time that Mass had been celebrated in Tenterden since the Reformation. The chapel was opened to the public, a school was started, and many baptisms took place over the next ten years. The priory was closed in 1877, and the community was transferred to Canterbury. After this, Mass was said by visiting priests in various locations, including a spell from 1891 onwards when a small iron building behind the present National Westminster Bank was used.

ST MILDRED'S CHURCH, INTERIOR 1900 45002

ST BENEDICT'S PRIORY 1903 44999

The priory has since reverted to its original name of Finchden.

HIGH STREET c1955 T24045

This shows the National Provincial Bank, originally the London and County Bank.

Perhaps the most significant addition was the building of the present St Michael's Church in 1863. The area had been known as Boresisle for many centuries – this was the name of one of the six 'boroughs' of the old Hundred of Tenterden. For some time, the curate of Tenterden, the Rev Seaman Curteis Beale, had been taking Sunday services in a wheelwright's shop, but things were soon to alter. His father, Seaman Beale of Finchden, bought land in the Ashford Road and built a school. He then built the church nearby, meeting most of the cost himself. Of distinctive design, the church immediately became a landmark in the area,

ST MICHAELS, THE CHURCH 1900 45006

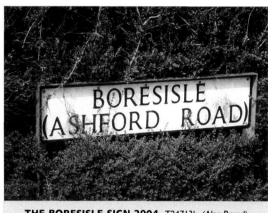

THE BORESISLE SIGN 2004 T24713k (Alan Brand)

whose name was changed from Boresisle to St Michaels to reflect the church's dedication to St Michael and All Angels. Many gifts from local parishioners allowed the new church to be furnished in a suitable manner. In 1884, a clock was added to the spire, followed by various other gifts during the 20th century.

Towards the end of the century, another feature was to be introduced into the life of the town: its own Directory. Jonathan Smith Thomson had come to Tenterden from Heathfield in 1837 to set up a business as land surveyor, living with his wife and family at East Cross Left before moving into the Manor House (ZZZ00011). After Jonathan's death in 1887, his son Walter started producing Thomson's Almanac, printing it in buildings to the rear of the house. The Almanac continued to be printed until 1940, from 1916 onwards by Walter's son, also named Walter.

ST MICHAELS 1900 45004

Did you know?

The Greens

Probably one of the better attractions in Tenterden for tourists, the Greens have been in existence for several centuries. But they took on greater importance when the turnpike road came in 1762 and houses were built both to the north and south of them. Later they were enhanced by a line of trees on either side, planted in 1871. The great storm of 1987 felled several, but there are still enough on which to suspend the Christmas illuminations every year. The Greens were for some time the location of the annual May Fair, and they have hosted such occasions as circuses and fetes.

THE OLD PITTLESDEN MANOR HOUSE 1912 ZZZ00011

(Reproduced by kind permission of the Tenterden Local History Society)

The printing of other publications continued until the latter's death in 1955, the last two years in Station Road. Miss Eleanor Frances Thomson also lived in the Manor and was well known for her garden and rose hedge. After Walter died, the house could not find a purchaser and was demolished - the site is now occupied by shops in Manor Row.

Thomson's Almanac was much more comprehensive in its information on Tenterden than its modem equivalent of the same name. It covered a variety of topics, such as advertisements by local shopkeepers and businessmen, and also some for national firms, along with a directory of private residences and their occupiers, commercial businesses, farmers and graziers - later on,

telephone numbers were added. There were details of all the churches in the town and their incumbents, with information on services, and of civic and associated bodies, including the Borough Council and the Tenterden Union (the workhouse). There was also information on markets, post offices, benefit societies and clubs.

The Almanac also gave details of public conveyances available, and a calendar and a diary. Similar information was also included for all the surrounding villages. Other miscellaneous but interesting items were included from time to time, such as accounts of holidays taken in Britain and abroad, short stories, and details of walks and cycle rides radiating from the town.

TENTERDEN c1965 T24081

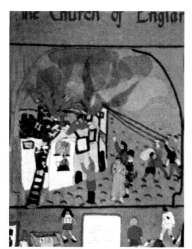

**THE COURT HALL FIRE,
THE TENTERDEN
TAPESTRY**

ZZZ00242

**THE SMUGGLERS,
THE TENTERDEN
TAPESTRY**

ZZZ00243

**THE TALLY-HO
THE TENTERDEN
MUSEUM**

ZZZ00244

(Reproduced by kind permission of the Tenterden Museum)

CHAPTER FOUR

The 20th Century

THE CENTURY began with the country still at war with the Boers in South Africa and an aged Queen Victoria coming to the end of her long life. In 1901, peace was restored on the African veldts; and after 64 years on the throne, Victoria died, to be mourned throughout the country, Tenterden joining in the feeling of loss. Her oldest son assumed the throne to become Edward VII - his coronation took place in 1902. The ceremony was originally planned

STEPHEN GOODSALL AS SERGEANT-AT-MACE ZZZ00164

(Reproduced by kind permission of Tenterden Local History Society)

Coronations and Royal Events

After King Edward's coronation in 1902, Tenterden celebrated three more similar events in the first half of the century. George V was crowned in 1911 with much ceremony nationwide and locally, including children's teas, sports and street parties. Following the turbulent year of 1936 when Edward VIII abdicated, George VI's coronation in 1937 was suitably honoured, again with the emphasis on children's activities. Elizabeth II came to the throne after her father's death in 1952; she was crowned the following year on a wet June day which restricted activities, but did not dampen the enthusiasm of the local people. In 1901, the Mayor of Tenterden as a Baron of the Cinque Ports had joined in the coronation ceremony, not now carrying the canopy over the monarch, but instead a flag of an Empire country: in 1953, Stanley Day was allocated the flag of Ceylon. Other royal events during the

century were the Silver Jubilee celebrations in 1935 for George V and in 1977 for Elizabeth II. George V is also recorded as visiting Tenterden; the Queen Mother visited too, to attend a K & ESR event. In 1990 Diana Princess of Wales opened the Leisure Centre.

CORONATION DAY 1911 ZZZ00163

Reproduced by kind permission of Tenterden Local History Society

for 26 June, but owing to his illness, it was changed to 9 August. Tenterden responded to the mood of the time and celebrated the event wholeheartedly. All the town's houses were decorated, and the shops closed for the day. Following a morning service in St Mildred's, all the townsfolk congregated in the Corporation Field (the Recreation Ground) to sing the National Anthem. They then paraded along the length of the High Street as far as West Cross, and returned to the starting point where a children's tea was held. The evening's entertainment was mainly open-air dancing, and it ended with a large bonfire and a fireworks display.

The Kent and East Sussex Railway

Starting as the Rother Valley Railway in 1900, and becoming the Kent & East Sussex Railway in 1903, the railway under Colonel Stephens served the route from Robertsbridge to Headcorn for over 60 years. Known colloquially as the Farmers' Railway, it served what was basically a rural area, and as such found it difficult to thrive financially. However, it was able to advertise in its timetable trains to and from London, changing at Headcorn, for the would-be visitor to the capital. Between the wars, various experiments in rolling stock were tried, such as mixed trains and the use of two Ford motor vehicles in tandem suitably adapted for rail operation. In 1948 it was nationalised along with the rest of British Rail, and the staff were dispersed to Ashford, Tonbridge and St Leonards. In 1954, passenger services were discontinued, and the line was freight-only until its closure in 1961. A number of enthusiasts managed to re-open the line on a limited scale in 1974, and since that time extensions to firstly Northiam and then Bodiam have been successfully carried out.

TOWN STATION, KENT AND EAST SUSSEX RAILWAY ZZZ00009
(Reproduced by kind permission of the Tenterden Local History Society)

The new century also saw the coming of a railway to the Tenterden area, after all the difficulties experienced during Victorian times. In 1900, a light railway was constructed from the South Eastern & Chatham Railway station at Robertsbridge, which terminated at what was designated Tenterden Station, near Ashbourne Mill. A few years later, the line was extended to the South Eastern & Chatham station at Headcorn; when Tenterden Town station was built, and the original station was renamed Rolvenden.

To increase the supply of public transport, there was a full-scale provision of buses in the area. As early as 1905, steam buses owned by the Headcorn, Sutton Valence & Maidstone Omnibus Co. were introduced to run three times daily from Maidstone to Headcorn, with the intention of extending the route to Tenterden. The return fares were much cheaper than on the SE&CR trains, which ran on a roundabout route via Paddock Wood. Unfortunately the company went into liquidation in 1908, and two further attempts by Kent Motor Services Ltd. that year, and by the Sutton Valence Steam Bus Co. in 1909, both failed; none of these companies managed to organise the extended service to Tenterden. But in 1912 petrol buses owned by the Sutton Valence Motor Co. laid on 3 return trips daily between Headcorn and Maidstone, supplemented by two additional trips to and from Tenterden. The First World War stopped any further expansion, but the immediate post-war years witnessed a veritable explosion of services. First in the field in 1921 was R & J Bennett & Co., who in addition to the haulage business, started to operate buses to and from Rye seven times daily. In 1923, a Mr Saxby started the Blue Car Motor Services based in the High Street with four buses; the firm was bought by Mr J E Brand in 1925, and ran buses over several rural routes in both the Tenterden and Ashford areas. By 1927, a direct daily service from Tenterden to London, as opposed to the previous necessity of changing to another London-bound coach at Maidstone, was operated by the Invicta Transport Co, which also supplied direct services to London from both Rye and Ashford. In the same year, a rival firm started up in competition – this was the Weald of Kent Transport Co based in Station Road. This company was destined to become the most successful one of the lot, and covered an extensive area of operation, as we can see in its 1927 timetable, (below). All buses were restricted to a maximum speed of 12 mph, and there are recorded instances of Weald of Kent

1927 Bus Timetable

Hawkhurst, Cranbrook, Tenterden, Ashford: 6 times daily, 3 times on Sundays.

Tenterden to Headcorn: 6 times daily, twice on Sundays.

Rye, Northiam, Hawkhurst, Cranbrook: 4 times daily, 4 times on Sundays.

Tenterden, Wittersham, Camber Sands: 3 times daily, 3 times on Sundays.

Tenterden, Woodchurch, Ashford: 6 times daily, 3 times on Sundays.

Headcorn, Pluckley, Ashford: 4 times daily, no Sunday service.

THE SPINNING WHEEL c1960 T24059

Edward VII's reign, although short in duration, was held to be a marvellous period for Britain as a whole, with its Empire 'where the sun never sets'. Tenterden had developed into a fairly prosperous town, with many traders flourishing. However, this affluence was offset by the number of poor who spent their lives in and out of the Tenterden Union (the workhouse), which was still functioning in Union Lane (now Plummer Lane). Despite the deterioration in the working conditions of the agricultural labourers in Victorian times, the town and surrounding countryside was still largely dependant on farming and its associated employment. May Fairs for sheep were held in late spring/early summer on the Greens (T24034 and 44990 page 83), with cattle fairs in September. Because of the mess on the Greens and the pervading smell, the fairs were moved to the Recreation Ground. The main motivation for the annual May Fair was the sale of sheep off the Romney Marsh and other neighbouring areas, which in earlier times had resulted in Tenterden's affluence thanks to the manufacture of broadcloth. Romney Marsh, and indeed areas nearer to the town such as the Smallhythe Levels, were traditionally damp flooded places before the complex flood relief schemes starting in the 1960s were implemented. A feature of the earlier part of the 20th century was the practice of removing flocks of sheep from those areas liable to floods to higher ground in the county, and even into Sussex. The exercise was known colloquially as 'keep sheep'; the farmer receiving the sheep usually looked after them from October to the end of the following March.

drivers being fined for travelling on the straight level stretch between Newenden and Sandhurst at such excessive speeds as 22, 23 and even 28.7 mph! Eventually all these companies were bought out by Maidstone & District, who by 1933 had monopolised the area, except for East Kent buses running in from Canterbury.

Excursion services in a variety of vehicles, including charabancs, were supplied by Mr Bourne of Woolpack Garage, C Dunster of Woodchurch, Dengate Bros. of Beckley, and E Harrison of Ashford. Additionally a motorised mail coach ran between Tenterden Town Hall and Ashford. The level of bus services continued throughout most of the century, until the popularity of the private car and deregulation in the 1980s resulted in only a limited number of routes being operated.

HIGH STREET c1955 T24034

HIGH STREET 1900 44990

BEACON OAK ROAD 1910 ZZZ00162

The gentleman carrying the pails of milk is Mr Albert Millen, a local farmer. At this date all milk was delivered to the door in this manner, at Tonbridge this procedure carried on right up to the Second World War and beyond.

(Reproduced by kind permission of Tenterden Local History Society)

Following Edward VII's death, George V was crowned in 1911 and assumed the role of monarch at a time of great unrest in the country and throughout Europe. Mrs Pankhurst with her Votes for Women campaign, Irish nationalism, and workers' discontent urged on by the Trade Unions, were all problems for the authorities, who had to use troops at times to quell trouble. However, Tenterden appears to have been little affected by this, being well-served by its shops and tradesmen, a comprehensive bus service, and trains to London and elsewhere from Headcorn. But within a few years, war was declared in August 1914, and the khaki-clad territorials were marching from the Town Hall to the station to travel to Dover and thence to France. Only two days earlier on the Bank Holiday the Recreation Ground had been full of people enjoying the annual fete, the races, the sideshows, and the fireworks. As the war progressed, soldiers from the Staffords, the Devons and the West Kents were billeted in empty houses, and sometimes the rumble of distant gunfire from France could be heard. At Leigh Green, a small airfield was completed in 1917, and RFC aircraft were a common sight over the town. At night Zeppelins could be seen on their way to London, picked out by searchlights located near Henley Fields and Pickhill.

Did you know?

Tenterden Cinemas

The first cinema in Tenterden was built in 1912 in Oaks Road, on the site now occupied by The Fairings. The original building still stands, and houses various shops and offices, including one belonging to Ashford Borough Council. It was a dingy place, unlike its successor, The Embassy , which was built in the High Street in 1937; the site is presently occupied by the Co-op. During the post-war boom in cinema-going, it was well used, featuring such films as 'The Bridge on the River Kwai', 'Henry V' and 'Doctor Zhivago'. The latter ran for 13 days, rather more than the usual 3-6 days of the others. Like many other cinemas throughout the country, it suffered from the rising popularity of TV, and it closed in 1969.

Right: **THE EMBASSY CINEMA c1955**   T24025a

Below: **OUTSIDE THE OLD CINEMA 1937**
ZZZ00166
(Reproduced by kind permission of Tenterden Local History Society)

THE MEMORIAL c1955 T24052

ASHFORD ROAD 1903 50998

This photograph shows Clifton House.

Education of the town's children during the 20th century was thoroughly catered for. The provision of state schools, which had been developed during Victoria's reign, was continued on a suitable scale, and enhanced by the addition of a school for 11-to 16-year-olds. In 1937, in line with County Council policy, thought was given to providing a Central School for 480 pupils, the building to be located in the Appledore Road. The onset of war in 1939 stopped that project, but in 1947 Lady Drury, the owner of Homewood, sold her mansion to the KEC rather than have it developed as a hotel or nursing home. The resultant school was started in 1949 initially as a secondary school, but in the 1970s it became a comprehensive. Private schools in the town, particularly during the early part of the century, were in their heyday. Opened during the period 1900 to 1918 were day and boarding schools, Beacon Oak High School (49077 page 89) and The Pebbles, and the Misses Blackman also ran preparatory classes for boys only. Assheton School at St Michael's Grange was a boarding school for boys aged 6 to 18 (49082 page 89), and Gatesdene in Elmfield was a 'high class home boarding school for girls'. All of these schools advertised a very comprehensive curriculum and prepared their pupils for many of the public examinations. Additionally, Assheton School claimed successes for boys who

BEACON OAK HIGH SCHOOL FOR GIRLS 1902 49077

passed Common Entrance examinations for several of the top public schools such as Charterhouse, Eton, Tonbridge and Uppingham. During the same period, Mr Villsher ran a commercial school at 30 High Street, and later Penderel in the Ashford Road opened its doors to boys under 8 and girls of all ages. In 1930, Petergate Preparatory School taught young boys before it moved to Petham near Canterbury in 1932, and smaller schools are recorded at Westcliff in Ashford Road, at Berwyn in Elmfield, at 2 Oaks Road and at Heronden. The majority of the private schools had closed before World War II, except Westcliff and Penderel, which was the last one in the town before its closure in 1970.

Despite the feeling nationally that war would not come again, and despite some backing for the appeasement of Hitler, Tenterden made provision for the worst before the outbreak of war in September

ST MICHAELS, THE GRANGE 1902 49082

This was Assheton High School for Boys from 1914.

1939. Arrangements were made for air raid precautions, the building of bomb shelters and the issue of gas masks. But little happened during the period of the 'phoney war'. Then in mid-1940 the skies were full of warring aircraft during the Battle of Britain. Later came the blitz on London and the awesome V1 'doodle bugs', and although the countryside was full of craters, fortunately only a few people were killed by enemy action. The town was outside the 10-mile restricted zone imposed before the Normandy invasion in 1944, but there were many noisy nights during which tanks and other military equipment were moved about to make the Germans believe that the Pas de Calais was the objective of the Allied landings. To assist in supplying the armed forces for this vast campaign, a pipeline under the ocean (PLUTO) was constructed; its route from the refineries went through the northern part of Tenterden.

For most of the war, Tenterden was full of service personnel, with the Divisional HQ of the Royal Signals at Homewood and that of the Royal Welch Fusiliers at Heronden Hall. With the Americans' entry into the war, USAAF airfields were opened at Great Chart, Smarden, Bethersden, High Halden and Woodchurch. Inevitably the town was full of Allied servicemen, and dances known as 'sixpenny hops' were arranged at the Town Hall. Records exist of Home Guard units being formed in Tenterden, including two special units (plus another one at Rolvenden) who in the event of German occupation of the area would have engaged in guerilla activity.

The relief at the finish of wartime activities with VE Day and VJ Day was celebrated with dances and outdoor events. Throughout the century, in addition to the various coronations, Tenterden people had always enjoyed

Pluto

When the invasion of Europe was being considered in 1943, thought was given to the provision of fuel for aircraft and military equipment after a successful landing had been achieved. To avoid the anticipated bombing of sea transport, it was decided to construct a pipeline under the ocean to the French mainland. Two routes were used to convey the fuel from the refineries: one went via the Isle of Wight to the Cherbourg area, the other through Dungeness to the coast near Boulogne. The latter route came from the Staplehurst area through Frittenden and thence to the north of Tenterden as far as Ingleden, where it turned towards the south through Pigeon Hoo, across Shirley Moor to Appledore, and followed the railway to Dungeness. In the event, neither route was used to a great extent - only 7% of the fuel used by the military went through the pipeline. There is, however, still evidence of its existence in the way of concrete troughing across streams, and near Dungeness sections of rusting pipes can be seen in the shingle.

themselves, as at the time of Silver Jubilees in 1935 and 1977, at the quincentenary in 1949 of the town's Charter, and at the 1951 Festival of Britain. The tendency was usually towards entertainments for the children, including tea parties in the streets, and sports on the Recreation Ground.

Sporting activities had indeed been developed during the 1900s, with a whole range of sports being supported. The town football club over the years enjoyed much success, both in league matches and area Cup rounds, and is still to the fore in the County League. The Cricket Club moved to is present ground at Morghew Park in Victorian times, and continued to expand its activities throughout the century; it entertained several illustrous XIs during that time, besides fielding teams including the Edmonds brothers - Phil Edmonds was the Middlesex and England spinner. The local golf dub, started in 1905 and located originally beside the Appledore Road, moved to its present course in 1925. It was expanded to an

TENTERDEN FOOTBALL TEAM, FINAL OF THE WEALD OF KENT CHARITY TROPHY 1972 ZZZ00261

The Tenterden football team carried off the Weald of Kent Charity Trophy on Good Friday, 31st March 1972 at Tenterden. Tenterden 2, Ashford Dynamo 0. Both goals were scored by E. Hobbs.

(Reproduced by kind permission of Tenterden Local History Society)

TENTERDEN CRICKET WEEK 1969 ZZZ00260 (Reproduced by kind permission of Tenterden Local History Society)

Tenterden v ARH Fullerton's XI at Tenterden, on Wednesday July 30th 1969, during Tenterden Cricket Week.
Back Row (left to right): John Kelly, Brian Johnstone, Phil Edmonds, Pierre Edmonds, Jack Gillett,
Graham ???, Colin Hopley (Umpire)
Front Row (left to right): Peter Lewis, Bob Wilson, David Jenner (Capt.), Bob McCallum, Chris Carruthers.

Tenterden 230 – 4 dec. (J R Gillett 85, R C Wilson 48, Ph. Edmonds 70)
ARH Fullerton's XI 105 (Ph. Edmonds 10.4 – 2 – 28 - 7)
Tenterden won by 125 runs.

18-hole course in the 1990s, and celebrates its centenary next year. On the Recreation Ground, a thriving Bowls club has existed for many years, and there are facilities for playing tennis nearby. Records exist also of a WI ladies' hockey team playing during the 1920s. Indoor favourites such as table tennis and darts have long been available, and the Leisure Centre (T24708k page 90), opened in 1990, allows participation in swimming, badminton and squash. In the early 1900s the town had a Goal Running club; Goal Running is a sport resembling the game of tag, which enjoyed great popularity in this part of Kent. For those keen to walk around the lovely Kentish countryside, a Footpaths Group, formed in 1968, is still a vibrant organisation with nearly 100 members.

THE LEISURE CENTRE 2004   T24708k   (Alan Brand)

Did you know?

The Festival of Britain

The Festival was produced by the Attlee government both to celebrate the centenary of the original one in 1851, and also as an attempt to rid the country of post-war 'blues'. The major events took place on the exhibition site on the South Bank in London, but Tenterden also had its own celebration during the fortnight starting 22 July 1951. Dame Edith Evans joined in the opening ceremony at the Town Hall - the participants had to endure heavy rain. Well-known authors such as Compton Mackenzie gave talks during the fortnight, and Gilbert Harding conducted a 'Twenty Questions' evening. Outdoor events included athletics, cricket matches and a horticultural show, whilst a tableau depicting William Caxton was well received: the Black Horse was renamed to honour this famous person.

HERONDEN HALL 1901 46368

As for religious matters, Tenterden gained two new churches during the 20th century. After many years of worship in different buildings, including a spell at Heronden Hall (above), a Roman Catholic Church dedicated to St Andrew was opened in 1934, a modern but distinctive building on Ashford Road (ZZZ00008). On the opposite corner of Turners Avenue, the Trinity Baptist Church was started in the 1970s.

Other developments during the century tended to be in line with national trends. For instance, in agriculture the smaller farms were bought up by larger organizations; examples are the present Sternberg Farms on the Appledore Road, and Morghew Park Farm, which stretches right down to Smallhythe - both cover hundreds of acres. Haymaking is done largely by machinery, as is the annual corn harvest. No longer are either carried out in a labour-intensive manner with men pitching onto wagons and thence onto stacks for later threshing. The combine harvester is now universal.

FROM SIX FIELDS c1955 T24048

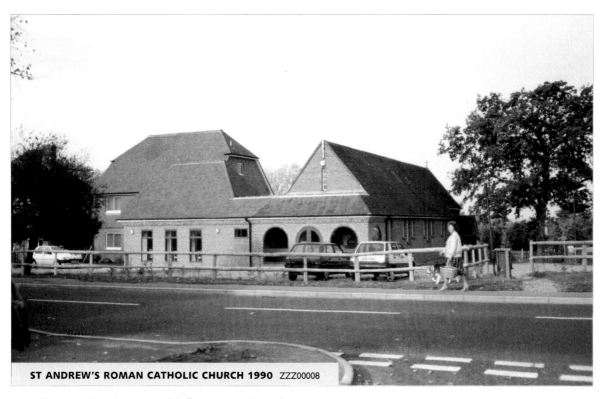

ST ANDREW'S ROMAN CATHOLIC CHURCH 1990 ZZZ00008

(Reproduced by kind permission of the Tenterden Local History Society)

In addition, hop picking is no longer done by manual labour in the hop gardens themselves, but by machines located close to the oast houses.

Another 20th-century change was that many local small shops such as grocers, greengrocers, bakers and butchers (examples can be seen in T24007, page 96) were gradually closed during the post-war years with the advent of the supermarket. Originally these were small affairs, such as Liptons, the Co-op and Brookeways, but in the 1990s Waitrose was opened, and it has been joined recently by Tesco. Housing development during the same period was similarly gradual: apart from a few small estates built in the 1960s and 1970s, building has been restricted to largely infill sites, so that the character of the town has not been spoilt.

The most significant feature of the century was probably the ending of the Tenterden Borough Council administration. With the implementation of the Maude proposals of the early 1970s, Tenterden could no longer be regarded as a Borough as from 1974. Instead it was placed under the newly-formed Ashford Borough Council, and the local council's powers were reduced to those of a parish council. However, as the legislation under the Local Government Act only conferred membership of the Cinque

HIGH STREET c1950 T24007

reciprocal visits were arranged. Following a temporary lull in these, attempts have been made to create greater interest in this idea.

Perhaps the town does cater more for the elderly retired folk in the form of the many organizations referred to in other sections of the book. This was balanced to a certain extent by the opening of the Leisure Centre in 1990: the activities available there attract children and younger adults. Outside the sporting clubs, there is very little for teenagers and the 18 to 30 age group to do, except perhaps to visit the occasional circus or fair when it comes to town; young people are more likely to spend their time in the various inns in the evening.

Ports Confederation on town and not parish councils, Tenterden Council promptly passed an appropriate resolution in the terms of the Act, so that the parish had the status of a town, and thereby had a Town Council with a mayor and councillors.

For the final quarter of the 20th century, Tenterden life was very calm, a reflection of its status as a small and pretty town. It had its celebrations, including the commemoration of the Queen's Jubilee in 1977, the 550th anniversary of the town's charter in 1999, and the Millennium in 2000. Other organised occasions were tried with varying success: for instance, a medieval banquet, an annual folk festival in October, and an attempt to revive the annual May Fairs. Perhaps one of the better efforts was the formation of a Twinning Association, in line with the national trend. The place chosen was Avalon in France, and over the years

Amongst the other developments which affected the lives of Tenterden people of all ages was that of the local surgery. A modern set of buildings carrying the name of Ivy Court in recognition of the old

OLD HOUSES c1965 T24087

house which stood for many years nearby, it is particularly well run, with a staff of six doctors, four sisters, and ancillary people such as dispensers and receptionists. One can usually obtain an appointment on a given day (far better than the situation in most parts of the country), and the availability of sisters for innoculations, blood tests and so on is a bonus. Special clinics include those for diabetics, early ones for commuters, and well woman clinics. Medical and nursing advice is also available on set days at some of the surrounding villages.

Another of the greater effects on late 20th-century life in the town was the increase in traffic control. Tenterden is bisected by the A28 from Hastings to Ashford, Canterbury and Margate. Parts of this route are quite rural, and the part through Tenterden, which includes all of the High Street in the town centre, is not particularly heavily used in comparison to other A-roads in Kent, or indeed the country. The exceptions to this are the times in the morning and afternoon when school traffic at Homewood and Recreation Ground Road causes queues of traffic. Before 1990, only one set of traffic lights regulated the flow of traffic – it was in the town centre near the Eight Bells. It is ironic that the coming of the two supermarkets brought about the provision of additional sets of lights; one set was erected at the end of Recreation Ground Road when Waitrose was opened, and the other the other more recently at the Smallhythe Road junction when Tesco was built. Both added to the successful regulation of traffic for the bulk of the day.

THE TOWN HALL 1955 T24038

CHAPTER FIVE

Present Day Tenterden

PERHAPS A REVIEW of the present-day Tenterden must start with the comparatively small amount of new building which has taken place, particularly in the town centre. After the considerable number of houses built during the 1960s in the St Michaels area and in other parts on the periphery of the town, there has been only a limited amount in the past 20 years, and that in most instances is infill of small sites. Ashford Borough Council, persuaded by such organisations as the Residents Association and (before its demise) the Tenterden Trust, and aided by the Town Council, have been very reluctant to give planning permission for new houses. This attitude has also applied to the construction of new shops, and indeed alterations to existing commercial premises. A proportion of the latter are listed buildings, and all come under the umbrella of the conservation area.

The exceptions have been the opening of branches of national supermarkets, Waitrose in the early 1990s (T24712k below) and more recently Tesco. The former was built on the site of a disused bus garage, and its arrival was generally welcomed by the townspeople. Tesco, on the other hand, met with quite determined opposition from some bodies in the town; it was eventually located on the site of the Kent Chemical Company. Both of these supermarkets, in different ways, plus the service offered by the local Co-op and a branch of Alldays, have generally met the shoppers' requirements. However, it must

WAITROSE SUPERMARKET 2004 T24712k (Alan Brand)

The Tenterden Vineyard

Following the considerable increase in wine drinking since the Second World War, the number of vineyards in Kent rose accordingly. Tenterden's contribution to that number is located at Spots Farm, Smallhythe, on the opposite side of the road to the church. The wines produced there have earned a reputation nationally, and several prestigious awards over the years. Visitors may while away the hours by going to the well-stocked shop and/or the cafe/restaurant on the upper floor. For the more energetic ones there is a vineyard tour, which includes visiting some of the buildings associated with the bottling, plus a walk around the vineyards themselves, passing a small rural museum en route. It is then time for the all-important wine tasting, and perhaps the purchase of a bottle or two. Alongside the main buildings is a herb centre, which also sells plants, compost, and so on, in the manner of a small garden centre.

be mentioned that their presence comes at a price: there are no greengrocers or fresh fish shops left in the town, and only one baker's and one butcher's still trading. It is hardly surprising, in view of the number of tourists visiting Tenterden, that there is an abundance of antique shops, fashion shops and cafes. Banks, building societies, estate agents and solicitors are prominent, and there are branches of national firms such as Boots, W H Smith and Woolworth's. The local Chamber of Commerce is well supported, and it is responsible for the Christmas illuminations in the High Street, plus the associated late night shopping evening in early December.

The town is blessed with a variety of organisations open to all ages, although in practice because of the high proportion of retired people in Tenterden, their members tend to be elderly. The Local History Society, founded in 1955, caters for those who are interested in the town's past, and the members enjoy talks during the winter months and outings to places of interest during the summer.

Tenterden has a town museum located in a stonemason's building off Station Road, run by keen volunteers belonging to the Museum Association, which was started in 1976. For those wishing to be more active and explore the lovely countryside around the town, there is a thriving Footpaths Group, which also arranges walks in other parts of Kent, and in Sussex. Keen gardeners can take advantage of the talks and outings programmed by the Local Horticultural Society, which also

THE FOOTPATH GROUP AT FIRLE IN SUSSEX 1990
ZZZ00167   (Alec Laurence)

organises shows throughout the year. For those interested in the finer things in life , there is a local branch of NADFAS, and also a National Trust Association, both of which arrange well-supported meetings on a regular basis. The Tenterden Lions are very active in raising money for good causes; the highlight of their year is the mobile carols which tour the town in December. As we have seen, Tenterden is fortunate to have a lively Residents Association, which attempts to ensure that local authorities encourage benefits to the town, at the same time campaigning against schemes which appear to be detrimental to it. For some time their efforts were supported by the Tenterden Trust, but that organisation closed recently and was merged with the Weald of Kent Preservation Society. Welcome additions brought about by their efforts have been the Town Sign (T24716k) located on the corner of Oaks Road, provided by the Residents Association, and the Town Map outside the Library, provided by the Weald of Kent Preservation Society. Both projects received financial contributions from other organisations in the town, as well as from private donors. There is also a Weald branch of the Association of Men of Kent and Kentish Men located in Tenterden, which arranges events in line with the county organisation.

All the foregoing organisations welcome members from all age groups, but there

THE BOTTOMS 1902 49078

THE TOWN SIGN 2004 T24716k (Alan Brand)

Did you know?
Tenterden Probus Club

Tenterden Probus Club for retired professional and business people was started in 1993 under the auspices of Rotary. The membership is open to both sexes, but at the present time there is only one lady member out of a total of over 50. For several years the club was located in the Vine Inn, but it was moved to the Eight Bells to allow an increase in membership. A recent move to Little Silver Hotel could result in a larger number of members in excess of the current limit of 60. The club meets on the first Thursday of every month for lunch, and on six occasions talks are given on a variety of subjects. Interesting outings to locations in Britain and Europe are arranged throughout the year.

are others which tend to be specifically for one generation. For the older and probably retired people, there is TENARA, the Tenterden Active Retirement Association. Social afternoons with games, quizzes and refreshments are organised, and outings are arranged to nearby places of interest. A week's holiday takes place annually to such localities as the West Country. Talks are arranged during the season, and all these events are well patronised by the members. For those wishing to be involved in more specific subjects, there is an active branch of the U3A, the University of the Third Age. A programme of talks and walking trips is supplemented by groups conducting research

into the town's buildings and its history. The less active elderly people are provided with facilities at the Day Centre, the building which in earlier days was the National School. Those who need transport to reach the building are conveyed to and from it in specially adapted ambulances driven by volunteers and provided with escorts. Apart from the refreshments available during the day, including lunches, there are helpers on hand that on given days will provide bathing facilities, hairdressing, chiropody, hearing aids, sedentary exercises and many other things. The Day Centre is run by a leader who receives great support from a band of volunteers. Not specifically for older

MOTHER'S UNION VISIT TO LAMBETH PALACE ZZZ00168 (Alec Laurence)

women, but in practice mainly supported by them, are the two all-female organisations, the Mothers' Union and the Women's Institute. The former are ladies associated with the church; as well as meeting monthly throughout most of the year, they support church activities such as making the posies for the children to hand out on Mothering Sunday and providing refreshments at flower festivals and other occasions. There are three Women's Institutes in the town: Tenterden WI and St Michaels WI meet monthly in the evening, and Tenterden Glebe WI meet in the daytime. In addition to the monthly talks, members take part in craft groups, music groups and sporting events such as walking, playing darts and short mat bowls. All three belong to the Tenterden District WI, which also arranges similar activities.

At the other end of the age scale, the families of pre-school children are catered for by playschools, including the Busy Bees, who meet in the Methodist Hall. For those who attend school during the day, there are Scout Groups based in Six Fields, and Girl Guides, with Cub and Brownie formations for the younger ones. A Youth Group has been in existence since the 1960s with its meeting place in Highbury Hall, which was built specifically for it at that time. The group caters for children between the ages of 7 and 11, and offers them the chance to participate in playing darts, snooker and indoor football. Older boys can play football in teams arranged by the local Football Club. There are, of course, organisations which may be supported by those in age groups between these two extremes, but not necessarily intended to be patronised by them exclusively. The Leisure Centre, opened in 1990 at the end of Recreation Ground Road, is such an example, with its facilities for swimming, gymnastics, badminton and squash. One can also take part in table tennis, bridge, aerobics, yoga, and chi ball, with courses in football, basketball, and trampolining. In addition, there is a health suite, a creche and a hall for hire. The Centre is well supported by people of all ages.

There are various sporting clubs which are still flourishing in Tenterden. The Football Club plays in the Premier Division of the Kent County League, using the Recreation Ground for their home matches. The Cricket Club, located at Morghew Park on the Smallhythe Road, fields teams most weekends of the season and enjoys a cricket week in August. The members of the Bowls Club play on the green on the Recreation Ground and participate in local leagues and in special events. The Golf Club with its 18-hole course is situated off the Woodchurch

TENTERDEN GARDEN OPEN DAY ZZZ00169 (Alec Laurence)

The Street Market

Apart from the May Fair for sheep sales and the September cattle fairs, Tenterden (unlike Ashford, Maidstone and Tonbridge) has not been regarded as a place where regular animal sales are held. But there is little doubt that since as far back as medieval times, a produce market has always been available for Tenterden folk to purchase goods. The medieval Market Hall was situated near the White Lion; it was demolished in 1823, to be replaced by a new building on the opposite side of the High Street (in 1896 this became the Fire Station). At the present time, the market stallholders themselves organise the weekly market, which is held every Friday throughout the year. For many years it was held in the Station Road car park, but because of falling interest, it was recently moved to the High Street, one section outside the Town Hall and a second one in the parking area near the National Westminster Bank. Unlike some local markets, the sale of clothing does not predominate; it is a more general market, selling cheese, eggs, fresh fish, bread, horticultural items and bric-a-brac. A farmers' market is also held one Saturday per month on the Recreation Ground.

HIGH STREET c1955 T24027 This photograph shows the new site of the street market.

Road. Other sports which may be played are tennis, on courts hired through the Leisure Centre, and pay-as-you-go golf attached to the London Beach Hotel.

To cater for both adults and children who are theatrically inclined, the Tenterden Operatic and Dramatic Society (TODS) is still in existence after many years, regularly arranging for plays and other entertainments to be put on during the year in the Town Hall.

Churches Together

Even in pre-1939 days, the seeds were being sown for a coming together of the Christian churches in the town. Since that time, and certainly during the past two decades, the Churches Together scheme has increased in intensity, and with success. The Lenten period has tended to be one of the more prominent times for this to manifest itself, with the holding of Lent lunches on Fridays at which each church takes it in turn to provide the food. On other occasions, a series of talks have been held at which the various incumbents, priest, vicar or minister, have spoken on matters relevant to Lent and Easter. Committees exist to organise these and other activities, and of course the Remembrance Day services are run by representatives of several of the town's churches. But perhaps the real example of the ecumenical spirit is when the incumbent of one church is invited to preach at another denomination's church.

Most years a play is entered in the county-wide competition for the best performance. Art is provided for by the Weald of Kent Art Club, which puts on an annual display of its work on the Recreation Ground. Other organizations include the Red Cross and St John's Ambulance and charities such as the RNLI. The nine churches in the town (three Anglican, one Catholic and five Non-conformist) each have their individual activities as well as church services. There are youth groups (in the case of St Mildred's, run by a professional Youth Leader), and women's organizations. Fetes and flower festivals are arranged, and under the auspices of Churches Together, Lent lunches are laid on, the proceeds going to Christian Aid.

The educational situation in Tenterden has been reviewed in the previous chapter; only state schools are available for children of 5-18 years of age. A nursery school exists at St Michaels for those below that age. The Infants and Junior Schools have maintained steady progress according to the Government's league tables, but it is Homewood School for those of 11 and over that has made the more dramatic progress. Its Sixth Form College section is expanding, with art and technology to the forefront of its activities. Recently the Sinden Theatre has been provided for use both by the students and outside organizations. It was opened by Sir Donald Sinden, the famous actor, who lives nearby; he is also a patron of the Barn Theatre at Smallhythe in the grounds of Smallhythe Place, once owned by Dame Ellen Terry (45008 page 108-9). Adult education courses are also available at Homewood, with WEA courses provided during the year, usually at St Andrew's Church Hall. For people in all age groups, the Public Library, as well as its book-lending section, has a Local Studies room, facilities for toddler reading sessions, video hire and use of computers. If one wishes to purchase books, a branch of Ottakar's has opened recently in the High Street.

SMALLHYTHE, ELLEN TERRY'S FARM 1900 45008

THE CEMETERY 1903 51007

Tourism is an important feature of Tenterden, especially since the opening of the Channel Tunnel, which has resulted in more foreign cars coming into Kent. The Tourist Information Centre, located in the Town Hall, provides a worthwhile service, although it is closed in the winter months. Pamphlets may be obtained for all the attractions in Kent and East Sussex, and overnight accommodation may be booked through the Centre. One of the greater attractions in the town itself is the Kent & East Sussex Railway, which despite some past financial difficulties is still running most of the year to and from Bodiam. Its Saturday night Wealden Pullman is still very popular with those who wish to 'dine with a difference', and the Santa Specials are a great hit with the children as Christmas approaches. Another feature in the town, especially popular with foreign tourists, is cycle hire, which may be used on the specially designated cycle routes such as No 18 to Tunbridge Wells, via the rural lanes. Most of the inns in Tenterden, in addition to the hotels, provide accommodation at reasonable rates, and B & B is available in the town and the surrounding countryside.

As we have seen, Tenterden has since 1974 been part of the Ashford Borough Council area, and it is that authority which provides much of its amenities. Weekly refuse collection and a specific recycling facility every fortnight are both provided by private contractors acting on the council's behalf. The council also maintains the local cemetery in the Cranbrook Road, which is having to be enlarged, despite the present tendency

Did you know?

The Millennium Garden

In line with the feeling throughout the country in 2000, thoughts in Tenterden turned to what could be provided in the town to celebrate this great Christian event, the start of the third Millennium. Several projects were proposed but discounted for reasons such as cost, but eventually agreement was reached on the provision of a commemorative garden. Despite its beauty, Tenterden lacked an open space where one might relax in a quiet atmosphere, and the area behind the Library seemed to have the potential for this. Accordingly, a garden was laid out on the site with a winding path, flower beds, grass areas and shrubs amongst its contents. Subsequent planting and care has allowed the garden to mature into a pleasant spot.

towards cremation. Street cleaning and the mowing of grass areas such as The Greens is generally satisfactory, but the removal of fallen leaves in the autumn on both this area and the pavements in the town is sadly neglected.

Tenterden's population has remained fairly static over the past decade or so, with house building being kept to the minimum. There is, however, a plethora of estate agents in the town, who maintain lively businesses selling the existing properties. But there is a measure of uncertainty now with the Government's avowed intention of increased housing in the Ashford area, the only cloud on the horizon for present day Tenterden, justifiably known as 'The Jewel of the Weald.

Far left: **THE RAILWAY, THE TENTERDEN TAPESTRY**
ZZZ00247

Left: **TENTERDEN TODAY, THE TENTERDEN TAPESTRY**
ZZZ00248

(Reproduced by kind permission of the Tenterden Museum)

THE TOWN SIGN 2004   T24715k (Alan Brand)

KENT COUNTY MAP SHOWING TENTERDEN AND SURROUNDING AREAS c1850

ACKNOWLEDGEMENTS

It is appropriate that I should acknowledge the part played by the late Hugh Roberts in my being in a position to compile this history of Tenterden. He left Tenterden in 1988 and I took his place in answering the family history and associated enquiries received from addresses both in the UK and overseas. Despite a tentative beginning, this started my interest in the town's history, and thereafter I was given constant encouragement by him to delve deeper and deeper, even from his home in the wilds of the North Yorkshire Moors.

Practical help in assembling the text and some of the associated photographs was received from Alan Brand, whose modern photographs are included in this publication, and Jack Gillett, both of whom are true Tenterdonians.

The co-operation of the Museum Association Committee and the Local History Society Committee in allowing the reproduction of photographs and illustrations (acknowledged in the text) is appreciated.

I must acknowledge the support and practical help received from my wife Joan, especially in the early days of planning the outline, and the subsequent compilation. Also to be recognised is the assistance given by our truly good neighbours, Glenn and Maureen Peacock, for proof reading when Joan was incapacitated in hospital after her serious accident.

Alec Laurence

BIBLIOGRAPHY

Tenterden, The First Thousand Years Hugh Roberts, 1995

The A H Taylor Manuscripts entitled Material Towards a History of Tenterden (Originals held by Tenterden Town Council; copies taken by the Local History Society, with permission)

History of Kent Hasted

The History of the Weald of Kent Furley

Francis Frith
Pioneer Victorian Photographer

Francis Frith, founder of the world-famous photographic archive, was a multi-talented man. A devout Quaker and a highly successful Victorian businessman, he was philosophical by nature and pioneering in outlook. By 1855 he had already established a wholesale grocery business in Liverpool, and sold it for the astonishing sum of £200,000, which is the equivalent today of over £15,000,000. Now in his thirties, and captivated by the new science of photography, Frith set out on a series of pioneering journeys up the Nile and to the Near East.

He was the first photographer to venture beyond the sixth cataract of the Nile. Africa was still the mysterious 'Dark Continent', and Stanley and Livingstone's historic meeting was a decade into the future. The conditions for picture taking confound belief. He laboured for hours in his wicker dark-room in the sweltering heat of the desert, while the volatile chemicals fizzed dangerously in their trays. Back in London he exhibited his photographs and was 'rapturously cheered' by members of the Royal Society. His reputation as a photographer was made overnight.

By the 1870s the railways had threaded their way across the country, and Bank Holidays and half-day Saturdays had been made obligatory by Act of Parliament. All of a sudden the working man and his family were able to enjoy days out, take holidays, and see a little more of the world.

With typical business acumen, Francis Frith foresaw that these new tourists would enjoy having souvenirs to commemorate their days out. For the next thirty years he travelled the country by train and by pony and trap, producing fine photographs of seaside resorts and beauty spots that were keenly bought by millions of Victorians. These prints were painstakingly pasted into family albums and pored over during the dark nights of winter, rekindling precious memories of summer excursions. Frith's studio was soon supplying retail shops all over the country, and by 1890 F Frith & Co had become the greatest specialist photographic publishing company in the world, with over 2,000 sales outlets, and pioneered the picture postcard.

Francis Frith had died in 1898 at his villa in Cannes, his great project still growing. By 1970 the archive he created contained over a third of a million pictures showing 7,000 British towns and villages.

Frith's legacy to us today is of immense significance and value, for the magnificent archive of evocative photographs he created provides a unique record of change in the cities, towns and villages throughout Britain over a century and more. Frith and his fellow studio photographers revisited locations many times down the years to update their views, compiling for us an enthralling and colourful pageant of British life and character.

We are fortunate that Frith was dedicated to recording the minutiae of everyday life. For it is this sheer wealth of visual data, the painstaking chronicle of changes in dress, transport, street layouts, buildings, housing and landscape that captivates us so much today, offering us a powerful link with the past and with the lives of our ancestors.

Computers have now made it possible for Frith's many thousands of images to be accessed almost instantly. The archive offers every one of us an opportunity to examine the places where we and our families have lived and worked down the years. Its images, depicting our shared past, are now bringing pleasure and enlightenment to millions around the world a century and more after his death. For further information visit: **www.francisfrith.com**

FRITH PRODUCTS & SERVICES

Francis Frith would doubtless be pleased to know that the pioneering publishing venture he started in 1860 still continues today. Over a hundred and forty years later, The Francis Frith Collection continues in the same innovative tradition and is now one of the foremost publishers of vintage photographs in the world. Some of the current activities include:

INTERIOR DECORATION

Today Frith's photographs can be seen framed and as giant wall murals in thousands of pubs, restaurants, hotels, banks, retail stores and other public buildings throughout the country. In every case they enhance the unique local atmosphere of the places they depict and provide reminders of gentler days in an increasingly busy and frenetic world.

PRODUCT PROMOTIONS

Frith products are used by many major companies to promote the sales of their own products or to reinforce their own history and heritage. Frith promotions have been used by Hovis bread, Courage beers, Scots Porage Oats, Colman's mustard, Cadbury's foods, Mellow Birds coffee, Dunhill pipe tobacco, Guinness, and Bulmer's Cider.

GENEALOGY AND FAMILY HISTORY

As the interest in family history and roots grows world-wide, more and more people are turning to Frith's photographs of Great Britain for images of the towns, villages and streets where their ancestors lived; and, of course, photographs of the churches and chapels where their ancestors were christened, married and buried are an essential part of every genealogy tree and family album.

FRITH PRODUCTS

All Frith photographs are available Framed or just as Mounted Prints and Posters (size 23 x 16 inches). These may be ordered from the address below. Other products available are - Address Books, Calendars, Jigsaws, Canvas Prints, Postcards and local and prestige books.

THE INTERNET

Already ninety thousand Frith photographs can be viewed and purchased on the internet through the Frith websites and a myriad of partner sites.

For more detailed information on Frith products, look at this site:
www.francisfrith.com

See the complete list of Frith Books at: www.francisfrith.com
This web site is regularly updated with the latest list of publications from The Francis Frith Collection. If you wish to buy books relating to another part of the country that your local bookshop does not stock, you may purchase on-line.

For further information, trade, or author enquiries please contact us at the address below:
The Francis Frith Collection, Unit 6, Oakley Business Park, Wylye Road, Dinton, Wiltshire SP3 5EU.
Tel: +44 (0)1722 716 376 Fax: +44 (0)1722 716 881 Email: sales@francisfrith.co.uk

See Frith products on the internet at www.francisfrith.com

FREE PRINT OF YOUR CHOICE
CHOOSE A PHOTOGRAPH FROM THIS BOOK
+ £3.80 POSTAGE

Mounted Print
Overall size 14 x 11 inches (355 x 280mm)

TO RECEIVE YOUR FREE PRINT

Choose any Frith photograph in this book

Simply complete the Voucher opposite and return it with your remittance for £3.50 (to cover postage and handling) and we will print the photograph of your choice in SEPIA (size 11 x 8 inches) and supply it in a cream mount ready to frame (overall size 14 x 11 inches).

Order additional Mounted Prints at HALF PRICE - £12.00 each (normally £24.00)

If you would like to order more Frith prints from this book, possibly as gifts for friends and family, you can buy them at half price (with no additional postage costs).

Have your Mounted Prints framed

For an extra £20.00 per print you can have your mounted print(s) framed in an elegant polished wood and gilt moulding, overall size 16 x 13 inches (no additional postage required).

IMPORTANT!

❶ Please note: aerial photographs and photographs with a reference number starting with a "Z" are not Frith photographs and cannot be supplied under this offer.

❷ Offer valid for delivery to one UK address only.

❸ These special prices are only available if you use this form to order. You must use the ORIGINAL VOUCHER on this page (no copies permitted). We can only despatch to one UK address.

❹ This offer cannot be combined with any other offer.

As a customer your name & address will be stored by Frith but not sold or rented to third parties. Your data will be used for the purpose of this promotion only.

Send completed Voucher form to:

**The Francis Frith Collection,
19 Kingsmead Business Park, Gillingham,
Dorset SP8 5FB**

Voucher for **FREE** and Reduced Price Frith Prints

Please do not photocopy this voucher. Only the original is valid, so please fill it in, cut it out and return it to us with your order.

Picture ref no	Page no	Qty	Mounted @ £12.00	Framed + £20.00	Total Cost £
		1	Free of charge*	£	£
			£12.00	£	£
			£12.00	£	£
			£12.00	£	£
			£12.00	£	£
			£12.00	£	£

*Please allow 28 days for delivery.
Offer available to one UK address only*

* Post & handling £3.80

Total Order Cost £

Title of this book . . . .

I enclose a cheque/postal order for £ . . . .
made payable to 'The Francis Frith Collection'

OR please debit my Mastercard / Visa / Maestro card, details below

Card Number:

Issue No (Maestro only):   Valid from (Maestro):

Card Security Number: Expires:

Signature:

Name Mr/Mrs/Ms . . . .

Address . . . .

. . . .

. . . .

. . . . Postcode . . . .

Daytime Tel No . . . .

Email . . . .

Valid to 31/12/16

Can you help us with information about any of the Frith photographs in this book?

We are gradually compiling an historical record for each of the photographs in the Frith archive. It is always fascinating to find out the names of the people shown in the pictures, as well as insights into the shops, buildings and other features depicted.

If you recognize anyone in the photographs in this book, or if you have information not already included in the author's caption, do let us know. We would love to hear from you, and will try to publish it in future books or articles.

An Invitation from The Francis Frith Collection to Share Your Memories

The 'Share Your Memories' feature of our website allows members of the public to add personal memories relating to the places featured in our photographs, or comment on others already added. Seeing a place from your past can rekindle forgotten or long held memories. Why not visit the website, find photographs of places you know well and add YOUR story for others to read and enjoy? We would love to hear from you!

www.francisfrith.com/memories

Our production team

Frith books are produced by a small dedicated team at offices near Salisbury. Most have worked with the Frith Collection for many years. All have in common one quality: they have a passion for the Frith Collection.

Frith Books and Gifts

We have a wide range of books and gifts available on our website utilising our photographic archive, many of which can be individually personalised.

www.francisfrith.com